From the Banks of Brook Avenue: Annotated Edition

complete text of
From the Banks of Brook Avenue
with author's discussion
of the origin
and development of the poems

W R Rodriguez

zeugpress

Dedicated to Mike Peterson, in gratitude for his technical advice and support of my publication projects over the decades.

Acknowledgments

Poems from this book previously appeared in the following magazines and anthologies: *And Justice For All; The Bronx County Historical Society Journal; Connections: New York City Bridges in Poetry; Dusty Dog; The Glacier Stopped Here: an anthology of poems by Dane County writers; Live Lines: Is There a Place for Poetry in Your World?; North Coast Review; POETS on the line; The Prose Poem: An International Journal; The Spirit That Moves Us; Tokens: Contemporary Poetry of the Subway; Welcome to Your Life: Writings for the Heart of Young America; You Are Here: New York City Streets in Poetry;* and *Z Miscellaneous.* The short poem, "genghis khan," by w r rodriguez, previously appeared in *Wormwood Review.* It serves as the basis for "yankee kitchen."

Cover Photo: *Glass Clouds* by Rob Rodriguez

© 2017 w r rodriguez
All rights reserved

Printed in the United States of America

ISBN: 978-0-9632201-7-2

zeugpress

Table of Contents

Preface and Introduction 5

from the banks of brook avenue: poems and commentary

I
forbidden places 9
a moon full and cold 12
just another new york city subway near death experience 19
yankee kitchen 22
the beach beneath the bridge 26
after seeing *night of the living dead* 29
on the coping 31
liberation: the brook avenue parking meter quartet 35
justice 39
she is leaving but 41
what could have more impact than a bus 44
plaza of the undented turtle 48
avenue b, 14th street, looking south 52
the push and break and chase of it 53

II
the third avenue el 57
standing upon the fordham road bridge 67
halloween 71
ne cede malis: poem for the seal of the borough of the bronx 76
washington comes to visit 79
grandfather: a photograph 84
bootblacks on the loose 86
al 92
p.s. 43 94
cypress avenue 104
skully 109
the tire man 114
a small but perfect world 117
the fountain of youth 120

III

welcome to the mainland 125
america's favorite pastime 138
yankee fan 141
the gambling leaguers 147
lost again on old subways 150
randall's island 153
triborough bridge: suspension 161
triborough bridge: stasis 164
triborough bridge: genesis 171
triborough bridge: kinesis 174
astoria park 177
the banks of brook avenue 180
Bibliography: Previous Publications 188

Preface

This *Annotated Edition* is for those, like myself, who are interested in the creative process. How does a poem begin? What images, thoughts, or feelings are in the writer's mind at its conception. And how does the poem evolve from idea to final form?

By revealing the people, places, events, and images from which the poems originated, I hope to give the reader insight into the creative process of transforming ideas, experiences, and imaginings into art.

This is a poet's "behind the scenes" view of his work.

So I will share the reality behind the poems.

A poem, after all, becomes its own reality.

Introduction to the Print Edition

The entire text of *from the banks of brook avenue* is included. Each poem is followed by *Author's Commentary* and *Author's Notes*.

Author's Commentary focusses on what inspired the poems.

Author's Notes looks at the evolution of the poems, and may include early notes or drafts.

The original type size and font of *from the banks of brook avenue* has been preserved.

Early drafts of the poems appear in a smaller type size.

How is a poem conceived? How does it evolve?

That is what this book is about.

I

…a wholly new ordering of ordinary affairs.

forbidden places

in all the forbidden places
like round the corner
and too far up the block
and up and down the you'll fall from it fire escape
and across the bad boy bad girl rooftops
of fertile pigeons and antenna thieves

through the sinister shadows of subway stations
and beware of dogs junkies
and the drunken super
basements
through the unexplored side streets of childhood
my mind wanders

that musk of the living
and dying tenement compels me
the gloom of alley and airshaft
the glow of sunlight on brick
i must navigate asphalt rivers
i must trek the broken glass

graffitied mainland to reach
the cement heart of the interior
and i will not return
i am the great explorer forever lost
in the concrete wilderness
i will discover america

flowering in the rubble

Author's Commentary: Initial Ideas and Inspiration

I do not recall that there is any one specific image that was the seed for this poem, but I do have a vivid memory of the basement of our tenement. Our kitchen, bathroom, and dining room windows overlooked the airshaft, a large open space that provided ventilation. I guess the airshaft was about fifty by one hundred feet, and the bottom, about sixty feet below the roof, never seemed to catch a sunbeam. The supers (building superintendents) had apartments in this gloomy underground world. It was a scary place to venture into: the staircase was constructed of old wooden planks on a metal frame, and one never knew what lurked down there.

Another image that comes to mind is that of an abandoned building near the garage where my father parked his car. The street was not wide, so we got a good view of the ground floor as we walked by. The building had not been boarded up; through the space where there had once been a window, I could see the darkened ruins of the front room, its charred walls, and the entry to another room behind it. A damp smell emanated into the narrow street. It seemed that the building had been made uninhabitable by a fire. I would never cross the threshold and explore the shadows beyond the broken door.

And there were other places I could not go. In the good old days people might sleep on tenement rooftops on hot summer nights or keep belongings in the basement storage room. Our mothers knew that the good old days were gone. They kept a careful watch on us. Our mothers let us play in the street, but we had to play where they could see us from the front window. And we usually stayed within our boundaries.

But the forbidden beckons, and the imagination wanders.

Author's Notes: Revision and Retrospection

This is an early version of the poem:

forbidden places (@ 1989)

in all the forbidden places
like round the corner
and too far up the block
and up and down the you'll fall from it fire escape
and across the bad boy bad girl rooftops
of fertile pigeons and antenna thieves
and through the sinister shadows of subway stations
and beware of dogs junkies and the drunken super basements
my mind has wandered
and not yet has found home

I liked the images in the original poem: fire escapes, shadowy subway stations, and rooftops where in the 1950s gangs sawed off television antennas to make zip guns.

However, I was not happy with the last two lines of the early draft. I played with the poem over the years. I have always been fascinated with Conrad's *Heart of Darkness,* which led me to the idea of exploring the urban wilderness. As I began contemplating the *from the banks of brook avenue* manuscript, I knew that this would be the opening poem. I did not want a poem that would be over a page long. I wanted a piece that would be understandable and that would lead the reader into the book. The reference to the "graffitied mainland" gently forshadows "welcome to the mainland," the poem that opens section III. I also wanted a positive end to the piece, thus the promise of flowers emerging from the ruins.

a moon full and cold

there was a moon full and cold
and i was a child in the big wide
unwanderable world
kept safe by my parents and warm
while the radiator with its ancient scales
of cracked paint hissed like a tame dragon

through the green forests
and brown fields of footworn linoleum
plastic soldiers advanced from their beachhead
to conquer the living room or to die in glorious battle
cowboys and indians skirmished at fort apache
alien spacecraft landed and robots ran amok

gallant knights with british accents
rode forth from castle walls to great adventure
fighting firebreathing worms and other strange creatures
so the countryside would be safe for travelers
and a child might sleep in bed and fear no harm
there was no gore just valor and victory and i

was general or prince or hero
anything is possible in the moonlight
this is the moon that shone over stalingrad
when death oozed through the rubble
this is the moon that glowed over the balcony
when romeo swore his love and juliet was enchanted

a leafless lifeless moon amid the tarpaper sky
which rose above the rooftops which shrouded our souls
shining white beyond empty streets and unlit windows
beyond unseen sleepers and reason and dream
a moon bright and distant
as a future as a friend as a life beyond the immediate

i pressed my nose to the windowpane and saw the moon
looming over lovers and battlefields
i wanted to sit forever in its light
to drink in the heavens to drown in wonder
ecstatic and enraptured
sated and thirsting for more

the fearless loveless bloodless moon
beyond the who and what and where of the sun's despair
its stark chill beckoned unanswerable

Author's Commentary: Initial Ideas and Inspiration

This poem originated in a childhood memory: One cold November night I peered out the window and saw the moon, so full and white against the black sky. The streets were quiet and empty. Perhaps that was the first time I ever really saw the moon. Or felt the moon. The image was embedded in my memory.

Perhaps its bright light made the darkness darker, and my loneliness lonelier, and perhaps I wanted to linger in the shadows.

The long days of summer were over. Summer offered the opportunity to play outside with cousins and friends. Fall, however, brought school, homework, early sunsets, and long, lonely evenings spent indoors.

I was an only child, without siblings to amuse and annoy me. But I did have many toys for entertainment. The mottled green and brown linoleum of the living room made an excellent landscape for all sorts of play.

And the radiator was near the window. And beyond was my bedroom. And my toy chest. And my toys. And the bed where I thought and imagined and dreamed.

Author's Notes: Revision and Retrospection

The poem originally began "once there was an old moon when once i was young / and smaller than I thought in a big wide world / a cold november moon hung amid the tarpaper sky."

As I worked to prepare the book, I learned that "old moon" could suggest a waning moon, and it was a full moon that enraptured me. The poem was set in November. As I learned from the *Farmers' Almanac,* it was not the Harvest Moon, nor the Yule Moon. The Full Beaver Moon did not seem to have the right ring to it. Hence "a moon full and cold."

The original draft mentioned loneliness: "a moon calcium and distant / as a future as a friend as a life beyond the immediate." Perhaps to wallow in this loneliness, I wanted to sit in a dark living room. This was referred to in the early drafts: "i wanted to sit in its black light / the fearless loveless bloodless moon / to drink in the heavens to fill my blood with night."

My parents never wanted to shut the living room lights off. Not when the television was on. Not even when the Christmas tree lights were on. Again, from an early draft: "such darkness forbidden among the unfortunately awake / there were rules to be followed and deaths to die."

These lines led in to a perverse despair: "i vowed to drown in snows which never came / i became a ghost with a child's polite smile."

About twenty-five years passed between the early draft and the final revision. I chose to create a poem with six line stanzas. I eliminated a lot of the despair and recalled the toys I played with. I loved my toy soldiers, and always regret reaching puberty and giving away the HO scale miniatures that I had collected from stores and penny gumball machines. I had a gyroscopic space ship. I had a monster called The Great Garloo, and a robot the name of which I cannot remember. Thanks to the internet, I could look up Fort Apache and see the log walls of its fort, the teepees, the cowboys, and the Native Americans. I still have the castle set; maybe I will take it out someday and set it up.

Before I had children, I played a fantasy game called Dungeons and Dragons. This led to an interest in military strategy games, many of which were produced by Avalon Hill. This eventually led to an interest in learning about World War II, and I read about the sieges of Leningrad and Stalingrad from books I borrowed from the library at the high school where I worked. I taught *Romeo and Juliet* to freshmen, three or four times a day, for over three decades, so I was very aware of the references to the moon in the balcony scene. The juxtaposition of the images of youthful passion and impassioned slaughter emerged: the moon over the carnage of frozen battlefields, and the moon as a backdrop for young lovers.

The despair present in the original draft is alluded to in the final piece: "beyond the who and what and where of the sun's despair," but the reference to the moon that precedes it is reminiscent of Keats' Ode to a Nightingale: "to drink in the heavens to drown in wonder / ecstatic and enraptured / sated and thirsting for more."

The original ending line to the first draft: "its crescent chill beckoned unanswerable" was flawed; it did not recall the image of a full moon. Finding a replacement for "crescent" made it more accurate: "its stark chill beckoned unanswerable."

an old moon: early notes (March, 1989)

once there was an old moon when once i was young
and smaller than i thought in a big wide world
a cold november moon hung amid the tarpaper sky
which loomed above the rooftops which shrouded our souls
white and full beyond empty streets

and tenements of stories of unlit windows
and unseen sleepers and reason and dream
calcium and distant
as a future as a friend as a life beyond the immediate
a leafless lifeless moon threatening winter
while the radiator hissed through its cracked paint
i played war on the linoleum and saw the moon
in my bones

an old moon (1989)

once there was an old moon when once i was young
and smaller than i thought in a big wide world
a cold november moon hung amid the tarpaper sky
which loomed above the rooftops which shrouded our souls
white and full beyond empty streets
and tenements of stories of unlit windows
and unseen sleepers and reason and dream
a moon calcium and distant
as a future as a friend as a life beyond the immediate
a leafless lifeless moon threatening winter
while the radiator hissed through its cracked paint
i played war on the linoleum and saw the moon
in my bones pressing my nose to the windowpane
looming over lovers and battlefields
i wanted so to sit in its black light
the fearless loveless bloodless moon
to drink in the heavens to fill my blood with night
such darkness forbidden among the unfortunately awake
there were rules to follow and deaths to die
i vowed to drown in the whiteness of snows which never came
i became a ghost with a child's polite smile
the disappearing moon
beyond the who and what and where of the sun's despair
the crescent chill beckoned unanswerable

an old moon (2008)

once there was an old moon when once i was young
a lone child in the big wide
unwanderable world
kept safe by my parents and warm
by the radiator which hissed like a domesticated dragon
through ancient scales of cracked paint

a cold november moon threatening winter
while plastic soldiers prepared for combat on worn linoleum
a leafless lifeless moon amid the tarpaper sky
which rose above the rooftops which shrouded our souls
stark white beyond empty streets and unlit windows
beyond unseen sleepers and reason and dream

a moon calcium and distant
as a future as a friend as a life beyond the immediate
i pressed my nose to the windowpane and saw the moon
looming over lovers and battlefields
i wanted so to sit forever in its black light
to drink in the heavens to fill my blood with night

the fearless loveless bloodless moon
beyond the who and what and where of the sun's despair
the crescent chill beckoned unanswerable

This 2014 revision is getter closer to the final version:

a moon full and cold (September, 2014)

there was a moon full and cold
and i was a child in the big wide
unwanderable world
kept safe by my parents and warm
while the radiator hissed through ancient scales
of cracked paint like a tame dragon

through green forests and brown fields
across the footworn linoleum
soldiers advanced from the doorsill beachhead
there was no gore
just valor and victory or death
and i was the general

or the prince or the khan or the centurion
anything is possible in the moonlight
this is the moon that shone over stalingrad
when death oozed through the rubble
and over the balcony when romeo swore his love
and juliet was enchanted

a leafless lifeless moon amid the tarpaper sky
which rose above the rooftops which shrouded our souls
stark white beyond empty streets and unlit windows
beyond unseen sleepers and reason and dream
in the moonlight all seems possible
santa claus will fly in its silver light

and beneath the stark sun the peasants sweat and toil
a moon calcium and distant
as a future as a friend as a life beyond the immediate
i pressed my nose to the windowpane and saw the moon
looming over lovers and battlefields
i wanted so to sit forever in its black light

to drink in the heavens to fill my blood with night
the fearless loveless bloodless moon
beyond the who and what and where of the sun's despair

its chill beckoned unanswerable

just another new york city subway near death experience

116th street and lexington avenue
three of us in the subway car
like some underground golgotha
when mister death walks in
not looking too kindly
we are not feeling immortal today
he is six feet tall he is five feet wide
he can sit anywhere he wants
but he stands right over me
cold eyes solemn mouth
in one hand a thick belt
dangles like a scythe
(the other holds the commuter strap
for proper balance because giants
do not like to tumble before their prey)
as the train rocks along
like the history of western civilization
which is irrelevant at this moment
of imminent doom
his eyes do not blink
his mouth does not smile
(i have lost my sense of humor
and all other sensation)
that immense hand
that mysterious belt
dangling in my peripheral vision
like a glimpse of heaven beyond pain
i cannot speak
i cannot run
the enormous gray clad arm
moves and the belt
taps my knee
taps my knee three times
his eyes do not move

i do not move
nor think nor feel
i have transcended
humanity in a subway tunnel beneath spanish harlem
and he walks off
to the next passenger
and taps his knee
three times then on to the next
three times and there are only three passengers
so he lumbers into the next car
searching for knees
and i feel like sir gawain released by the green knight
introspective and glad to be alive
i am young and i have learned
that experience is not unique
that the inevitable is
sometimes avoidable though i don't know how
and that for a mere fifteen cent token i can wander
forever searching for the man who taps knees
but when a voice says *shoot boy it was just another*
new york city subway near death experience
i remember that i was going to play basketball and maybe
talk to some girls afterwards though i am
a lousy shot and terribly
socially awkward

Author's Commentary: Initial Ideas and Inspiration

I can still see him standing over me. Maybe he was not five feet wide, but he was pretty big. He looked down at me, and I up at him. He tapped my knee, three times. And did the same to the other two passengers. And left. Just who was that mystery man? What was his fascination with knees? The number three? I will never know. I prefer not to meet him again.

Author's Notes: Revision and Retrospection

I do not recall any great struggle from early draft to final. Perhaps that is because the poem tells a story. The beginning sets the scene and creates the mood. The plot opens with a suspenseful scene: he stands over me; what will he do? Fortunately for me, not much is going to happen in the plot.

How the story is told is important. The suspense created by the threat of the dangling belt is lengthened by the parenthetical comment, and also by the statement that "the train rocks along / like the history of western civilization." To my great relief, the guy just tapped my knee three times and walked off.

I hope that the short lines and the details of his action and my inaction effectively create in the reader the fear that I experienced. And I hope that the reader shares the "comic relief" suggested by: "I have transcended / humanity in a subway tunnel beneath spanish harlem."

Fortunately for all three of us, the gentleman in the gray sports coat completed his ritual and left, presumably looking for more knees. From my viewpoint, this was a most happy ending.

But it is anti-climatic. The story may be over, but the poem is not. I could not ignore the comparison of three knee taps with the three ax blows the Green Knight bestows on Gawain. Great heroes are transformed by their quests, but I was a young teenager on a subway train beneath Spanish Harlem: "i have learned / that experience is not unique / and that the inevitable is somehow avoidable / though i do not know how." But certainly every fifteen-cent token brings the promise of a new adventure!

It has been about fifty years since this happened. I do not remember if one of the passengers said "shoot boy it was just another / new york city subway near death experience," or if I made it up. I hope it was a direct quote.

yankee kitchen

there are paintings of quaint towns by the sea
and clippers slicing windswept waters
wood trim and white bricks
a touch of new england in new york
with a whiff of chowder on the menu
harbored next to a massive gray church
where angels watch over the world
and the monstrance shines over the globe
and the winged herald on the corner wields a trumpet
louder than all the taxicabs on lexington avenue
if only we could hear it
but we sail the winds and waves of adolescence
and drift back to this modest diner
with its patina of grease and nicotine
to listen to ourselves and feast
upon just being friends
in that delicious time
before the future pulls us apart
and we become like the pedestrians beyond the window
scurrying to love to money to fashionable
restaurants or dive bars
honking like traffic at anything in the way
some of us will make the angels cry
some will just wander off
into life but for now
we have nothing to do but sit
together and sip our sodas until the ice
turns to water while ralph
the aged waiter with the patience of a saint
lean and drawn like the farmer in *american gothic*
and a loving smile pretends not to see
jerry use his straw to shoot spitballs at the good
citizens of nantucket so purposefully
portrayed in oil amid the rustic wooden frame

while in the infernal heat of the kitchen
the anonymous infamous fry cook grills
hamburgers cheeseburgers and anything we can afford
we do not know his name but we call him
genghis khan because legend has it he once
charged from the grill waving a butcher knife
at a customer who complained
so we laugh and to the last
lick of grease eat clean the bone
white plates of our hungry
youth

Author's Commentary: Initial Ideas and Inspiration

The poem began as a very short piece (nine lines) called "genghis khan," based on the rumor that an angry, knife-wielding cook threw out a customer who did not like the food.

Yankee Kitchen was next to St. Jean Baptiste Catholic Church at 76th and Lexington. I was in a Boy Scout troop at St. Jean's, and I was friends with kids who went to school there. We played basketball in the gym and punchball in the courtyard. Too young to hang out in the local bars, we refreshed ourselves with burgers and sodas. Yankee Kitchen was our place, in a time when we were still young and relatively innocent.

I built the poem on top of the Genghis Khan image that would form the ending. This seemed strangely appropriate: for five years I had an office job at Saint Anne's Shrine, which was in a building adjacent to the rectory. Eventually, the church closed the building and sold the property. The facade of the office building was kept, and a high rise erected above it.

Author's Notes: Revision and Retrospection

In 1993, the short poem, "genghis khan," appeared in *The Wormwood Review:*

genghis khan (1993)

genghis khan
we secretly named him
the anonymous infamous cook
of yankee kitchen restaurant
charges from the grill waving a butcher knife
at customers who complain
while we laugh
and to the last lick of grease
eat our plates clean

As I was planning *from the banks of brook avenue,* a poem about Yankee Kitchen was on my list of possible ideas. The restaurant is no longer there, so I tried from memory to recall its decor. I remember the painting of the sailing ship, and of a town, which I presume to be Nantucket. I do not know if clam chowder was featured on the menu, but it would seem to fit the restaurant's theme.

Saint Jean Baptiste Catholic Church is now a historical landmark. It is a beautiful church, with an abundance of stained glass windows (not mentioned in the poem) that were created in Chartres. As a teenager I did not appreciate its beauty, nor was I thankful enough for the kindness of the Blessed Sacrament priests and brothers who let me, a kid from The Bronx, into their Boy Scout troop, who eventually employed me as a clerk, and who let me play in the gym with my friends.

Thanks to the internet, I could view images of the church, and I focused on the statues over the main entrance. At the corner of 76th and Lexington, the "winged herald" still "wields a trumpet," but as teenagers we probably only heard the honking horns of the incessant traffic.

I try to capture a time of innocence, "that delicious time," when our worst offenses were throwing snowballs or shooting spitballs at paintings. As we sailed "the winds and waves of adolescence," we wandered off into life, and I could see that some were going in directions that would "make the angels cry."

And thanks to the internet, I could view the *American Gothic* painting. Ralph was not an exact replica of the dentist, but he was tall and skinny, with a "lean and drawn face." Claiming that Ralph had "the patience of a saint" may be an exaggeration, but he never asked us to leave.

And, more importantly, he never asked the cook to ask us to leave.

the beach beneath the bridge

a strip of sand and stone
between overgrown grass and gray water
white suburban homes mottle the leaves
of a distant shore
thirteen years old our footprints
are pools in the mud
we walk away
from parents and baseballs
there are mussels and driftwood
a horizon and a sky
ashes of bonfires burnt out
like the passion of night's lovers
the beach is awash with a love we barely understand
the smell of lowtide mud and brine
there is no going back not yet
the uncertain future ebbs and flows
now beneath the bronx sun we run and laugh
and stumble in the cold dark waves

Author's Commentary: Initial Ideas and Inspiration

This poem began as a memory of a place: Ferry Point Park, which is by the Whitestone Bridge. On one side of the bridge was a shoreline of rubble, where my father once took me fishing. On the other side was a field and a small strip of beach. One day my parents took took me and a friend there to play. We wandered from the field and walked on the sand, getting our feet wet in the waves.

Along with the shells, stones, and driftwood, there were many white circles. At the time, I did not know what they were. Eventually I realized that at night the park was a spot for lovers to meet. The poem tries to capture a time of transition from innocence to awareness.

Author's Notes: Revision and Retrospection

This memory was originally the opening to "ferry point park," which appears in *concrete pastures of the beautiful bronx*, but I decided to make it a separate piece. By separating "beach beneath the bridge" from "ferry point park," I was able to give a sharper focus to the two distinct themes: "beach" captures a moment in early adolescence; "ferry point" portrays a father and son memory grounded in a particular time and place.

I am writing these comments in 2017 about an event that occurred in the early 1960s. Our culture has changed. When I was young, feminine hygiene products, birth control devices, and male enhancement products were not advertised on television. On *The Dick Van Dyke Show*, Robert and Laura Petrie slept in separate beds. So perhaps that puts our finding of what Lenny Briscoe on *Law and Order* refers to as "Coney Island starfish" in perspective. Recalling that time of long ago, it seems accurate to say: "the beach is awash with a love we barely understand," and to end the poem with the image of stumbling "in the cold dark waves."

These are some notes from my 1988 notebook:

beach beneath the bridge notes (7/11/88)

at twelve years old we ran fields
and hopped barefoot over the rocks
and through the cool sand
the rings of disintegrated condoms
washed on the beach like sand dollars

beach beneath the bridge notes (11/9/88)

the beach beneath the bridge
a strip of sand between the breeze blown grass
and the dirty waves

the suburbs beyond the water
we walk away from
parents and baseballs
across the muddy sand
there are driftwood and mussels
a horizon and a sky
a smell of something almost natural
the wind calls us to our future
rings of condoms
litter the beach
like pointless starfish
ashes of bonfires burnt out like a passion
but today we are just pirates

Looking back on these notes, "the suburbs beyond the water" and "a horizon and a sky" are ideas that were put into "ferry point park," as such:

> "but the horizon is the whitestone bridge
> a turquoise arch suspended overhead . . .
> which crosses even the sky
> to the green suburban shores
> of queens beyond unswimmable waters"

The photograph of my fishing from the rocks became the cover of *concrete pastures of the beautiful bronx*.

I do not have a photograph of the treasures we found on the beach beneath the bridge, nor do I want one.

after seeing *night of the living dead*

stiffarmed we limp across the commons
they're coming to get you barbara
we yell from dormitory bushes
on this hallowed ground
where edgar allan poe
once haunted the jesuits
but no one is scared so we
stagger into the pub to bend
our elbows till dawn
pretending to be
cinema heroes and poets
and in the platonic light of day
when we are only ourselves
they up and run
premeds
junior accountants
student politicians
literally up and run
they conform so well
we not at all
they will flourish and prosper
we will write and paint and teach
and grow old paying bills
starving for the days
and nights when we
roamed the gothic campus
young alive hungry
liberal arts
rebels

Author's Commentary: Initial Ideas and Inspiration

Yes it really happened. I went to Fordham University in The Bronx. One night A few buddies and I went to see a campus showing of the black and white original version of *Night of the Living Dead.* During a particularly scary scene, I reached around and pinched the neck of one of my friends. He jumped three feet straight up in the air. I did not put that in the poem. Afterwards, we wandered around for a few minutes reenacting some of the movie scenes. I guess we were the weirdos and not held in great esteem by the more conventional types. But, hey forgive me, I was an English major.

Author's Notes: Revision and Retrospection

The original version emerged rather easily, but made no reference to Poe. I remember seeing *The Raven,* starring Vincent Price, Peter Lorre, Boris Karloff, and Jack Nicholson, shown outdoors on one of the lawns of Fordham University. Quite a cast, and quite an appropriate location to view the film.

As I used the internet to research material for my manuscript, I came upon an article, "Edgar Allan Poe and the Jesuits" by historian Dr. Pat McNamara (*Patheos:* October 31, 2011). Poe often walked the grounds of St. John's College, now Fordham University. Poe's wife died shortly after their move to The Bronx, and the grieving widower often joined the Jesuits for dinner, cards, conversation, and consolation.

Poe's Cottage has been preserved and restored; it is not far from the Fordham campus.

on the coping

atop the parapet
of a five story walk-up
on the outer edge
of coping

he stands
fifty feet in the air
upon the smooth
downward slope of tile

his kite soars
a soul
in search of heaven
and he smiles

childhood stops
children gaze
with upturned
wondering eyes

there must be angels
in the clouds
a miracle flutters
overhead

the eternity
of a summer afternoon
the immortality of youth
the timeless awe

those black sneakers
on the brink
of doom
and suddenly

a jump
a blind
backwards leap
onto the tarpaper roof

the kite
sports in the wind
and he descends
creaky stairs

to the rest of his life
to be found years later
jaundiced
needle scarred

dead in the stench
of an unlit doorway

Author's Commentary: Initial Ideas and Inspiration

The image of this young man casually standing on the edge of doom has stayed in my mind for many years.

Coping is a tile atop the parapet or short wall that lines the roofs of many tenements. The coping has a peak in the middle; half of it slants inwards towards the flat roof; the other half slants outwards towards the emptiness beyond. This teenager was standing on the outer edge and flying a kite.

We were kids. We watched. At the time I probably thought something like: "Wow. If I could get up on the roof I probably could get my kite that high up in the sky." When I worked on the final revisions of the poem, I almost shuddered at the horror of the scene.

Author's Notes: Revision and Retrospection

An earlier version appeared in *Dusty Dog:*

on the coping (1993)

on the outer edge of coping
he stands atop the roof's parapet
between ungraspable father sky
and the concrete skin
of mother earth which buries all
where we play punchball in the afternoon
beneath ruddy tenements
on the irish side of the street
but stop to watch
those black sneakers
on the downward slope of chocolate tile
scarred arms righting the kite
in a wind which does not blow
on the children below
he stands curbside casual
a jaundiced junkie face
turned toward the clouds
and the heavens so far away
his sneakers but a hundred feet above
certain death
the kite flies like a soul it seems for an hour
till he turns from a mythic fall
to walk back into his pedestrian life
to be found years later
dead in the stench of an unlit doorway

The revision changes the opening to focus on details of the danger. The tenement roof had a low wall, a parapet, topped by saddle coping, in this case, smooth tile which sloped downwards in two directions and which peaked in the middle. I calculated his height above street level by multiplying the five stories of the tenement by ten. He was actually on the side of the building, not the front, and if he fell he would have landed on the roof of the W. T. Grants five and dime. Such a fall could be fatal.

I also added more about the children watching. I could not resist echoing Romeo's lines from the balcony scene, where Juliet, being over his head, is as glorious as an angel bestriding the clouds over "white-upturned wondering eyes." But we were watching neither an angel nor a thirteen-year old girl ensconced on her balcony; we were fixated on a reckless teenage boy standing on the edge of death with the casual demeanor one might have standing on a curb waiting to cross a street.

I also chose to echo Blake's "The Chimney Sweeper." The untethered kite that "sports in the wind" recalls Blake's chimney sweeps who posthumously "rise upon clouds, and sport in the wind."

liberation: the brook avenue parking meter quartet

I
the war droned
air america
deathdrugs
slumlord decadence
nightsticks and headblood

nor freedom from ourselves
eternities of tenements
work
sweat
survival

rentstrike
riot
petition
so many nouns and verbs
yet the poor are always among us

II
the resignation
of sun on concrete
the protest wind
of winter apartments
life is the struggle to live

brook avenue is indifferent
to saint and thief
time and space are money
taxation inevitable
and the city will take its tithe

we labor we sleep we dream
we awaken to parking meters
parking meters on brook avenue
where the sewerburied stream flows
invisible as hope

III
where orchards once grew
now stark
silver moneytrees
eat the fruit of our labor
we pay to park and we pay

for the means to make us pay
coinboxes are stolen
and we pay for replacements
by day we spend
by night we are robbed

dime by thin roosevelt dime
from weary hands
our wealth trickles
through treacherous currents
to the ocean of greed

IV
midnight's entrepreneur
is an invisible
lumberjack
hacking a trail of steel stumps
through urban wilderness

a cycle of thievery
and fruitless reforestation
meters reappear
to disappear again
and again and again

and again until
the city withdraws
from this war of attrition
no more parking meters
no more parking meter thief

the avenue is free
as a babbling brook

o liberation

Author's Commentary: Initial Ideas and Inspiration

Parking meters were installed on Brook Avenue. A mundane event, perhaps, though it was interesting to see that the money boxes had been neatly removed from the very sturdy poles.

Brook Avenue, as I learned from research, follows the course of the millstream and was subsumed by the construction of the street. The brook is now part of a sewer. The virgin wilderness of the South Bronx passed from the Native Americans to Jonas Bronck; it became Morris Manor, which included orchards and collections of trees.

There were no trees on the block where I grew up, but, with a sarcastic imagination, I could envision parking meters as "money trees" and the thief as a "lumberjack."

This attempt by the city to squeeze a few more dimes out of the neighborhood was happening as the South Bronx was deteriorating.

A guerilla war, perhaps an urban parallel of the Vietnam conflict, but fortunately not as deadly.

Author's Notes: Revision and Retrospection

Nouns and verbs, objects and actions, are the most important words in a poem; the words that describe them, adjectives and adverbs, are the second most important. Nouns and verbs comprise images, and one way to construct a poem it to offer images to the reader. These ideas, I think, are reflected in the sparse lines of this poem.

A music aficionado may not approve of my use of the term "quartet." I am not well schooled in music. To me, "quartet" suggests an elegant treatment of a worthy subject, and this poem is about hard times and petty crime in the South Bronx: the tone of the title contrasts the content.

I love sarcasm and irony, which is suggested in the main title and last line of the poem: "liberation."

justice

a youth grabbed an old woman's purse fat with tissues and aspirin and such sundries as old women carry in sagging purses a desperate youth nice enough not to beat her head bloody into the sidewalk as muggers of the feeble often do for the fun of it i suppose and he ran up the hill but one of the perennial watchers watched it all from her window the purseless old woman in slow pursuit yelling such curses as it takes old women a lifetime to learn but it was too dangerous too futile the silent watcher knew to call the police who might come and rough up someone they did not like just for the fun of it i suppose or who would talk polite and feel mad inside and roll their eyes because there was really nothing they could do and there were murders and assaults to handle so this silent angry watcher carelessly but carefully dropped flower pots from her fourth floor windowsill garden one crashing before one behind and the third hitting him on the head a geranium i suppose and closed her window while the huffing grateful old woman looked up at the heavens to thank the lord and when she finally calmed down she walked off with her purse laughing and leaving the youth to awaken in the blue arms of the law and do you know two smiling cops walked up all those stairs to warn the watcher that if she weren't more careful with her plants she would get a ticket for littering i suppose

Author's Commentary: Initial Ideas and Inspiration

I heard that a woman got mugged and another woman tossed a flower pot from her window and hit the mugger on the head.

I believe this happened on 135th Street. It was the age before reality television, so people did sit at their windows to watch what was going on. And window sills were good places for flower pots.

I do not know if the police were called, but if they were, I imagine that they might have found some dark humor in the quick administration of justice.

Author's Notes: Revision and Retrospection

The poem is written without punctuation, and there are no line breaks to establish breath groups, so my task was to create a rhythm that would carry the reader along while telling a logically coherent story. The repetition of sounds and of words is important to the flow of this poem. In an unpunctuated prosepoem such as this, conjunctions organize the story and contribute to the rhythm.

The repetition of "i suppose" helps organize the poem. The phrase seemed appropriate as I was writing about an event I did not directly observe. It conveys a world-weary attitude, an acceptance of the outrageous or the absurd. It seemed to make a fitting end to the poem: "if she weren't more careful with her plants she would get a ticket for littering i suppose."

This is a very early rough draft:

justice (1990)

he grabbed the old lady's bag as she walked beneath an overpass built by the wpa when thugs were thugs and the government was a friend as even today we like to believe and babe ruth still played baseball and the world was wonderful except for stuff like hunger fascism racism purges and polio but at least in the bronx you could still leave your door open all night so the milkman could deliver right to the icebox if you could afford milk and since no one had much anyway it was easy some sunday night to move after the "two months rent free" expired and before the bill was due to move to another "sixty day free stay" (and she had survived all that) and movies were still a nickel where you could also leave your door open because the poor are proud even when they are hungry and movies were still a nickel as we had heard so many times and this old lady danced with soldiers in times square at the war's end and gave birth during the korean war and sent her sons to vietnam and grew old and gray while they married and divorced and lost jobs and melted into the streets and was enjoying the peace of this afternoon lugging her shopping bag when this kid grabbed her bag

she is leaving but

she is leaving but
pauses a moment
before the great
overhead thud
our upstairs neighbors
like to play so they wrestle
the burly father
the burly son
and the takedown
takes down the ceiling

my amazed aunt had turned to talk
stopped at the french doors
on the threshold of doom
by mundane words
a second before bricks
and whiskey bottles
left by turn of the century
italian plasterers
and genuine italian plaster
crash in a dusty thud

she laughs to see
a leg poking through
she laughs to be standing
in our living room
an oasis with green sofa and chair
art deco end tables and console television
she laughs just to be alive
in a rent controlled apartment
in the south bronx
where no one escapes death

and she laughs

Author's Commentary: Initial Ideas and Inspiration

My aunt could have been killed by the falling debris. She had almost entered the dining room, but stopped at the French doors to talk a bit more. Just a moment before the dining room ceiling collapsed. Plaster chunks are heavy, and there were a few bricks and bottles left in the ceiling by whoever made it. I did not see the leg poking through, but I think my aunt did. Sadly, she died of cancer a few years later.

Author's Notes: Revision and Retrospection

The earlier version was shorter:

she is leaving but

she is leaving but
the ceiling falls
the obese father
wrestles his obese son
half our dining room
ceiling crashes
my amazed aunt
had turned to talk
just a bit more
stopped on the threshold
of doom by mundane words
a second before bricks
and whiskey bottles
left by turn of the century italian plasterers
and genuine plaster
crash in a dusty thud
she laughs to see
a leg poking through
she laughs just to be alive
in the bronx where no one
escapes death

Sometimes the idea for a poem falls right into one's lap. Fortunately, my lap was in the other room at the time.

Our tenement was built in 1906, and I think the buildings were well constructed. But plaster ceilings do crack and develop weak spots, and the ceiling was over fifty years old at the time.

The simple story is this: the ceiling collapsed in front of our eyes. Turning a simple event into a poem is the challenge.

I came up with the line "she is leaving but" early in the process. Ending the line with "but" seemed to add a touch of suspense and to set up my aunt's pausing and turning at just the right moment.

The short lines also seemed to work.

I cannot document that the plasterers were Italian, but my Irish mother-in-law did point out that her father could not get work in the trade because he was not Italian. And I am half Italian. So I made the plasterers all Italian.

As I was working on this *Annotated Edition,* I learned that lath-and-plaster ceilings, common at the time the tenement was built, probably used lime plaster, which is also known as Venetian or Italian plaster. So I am changing "and genuine plaster," the line that appeared in earlier editions, to "genuine italian plaster." The repetition seems to complement that used in the first and third stanzas.

The final version includes a few details about our living room: "an oasis with green sofa and chair / art deco end tables and console television." This was the place where our family often gathered. With four sisters living on the same block, there was plenty of family. So the family gathering places were little havens of love and stability in a changing world

Adding "and she laughs" as the last line gives a sense of the joy of life: laughter, too, is an oasis of sorts.

what could have more impact than a bus

what could have more impact than a bus
boasted the bus on a bus long fluorescent sign
advertising advertising space along the roof
of this new bus and its new bus brethren
who bore the plastic banners of big corporations
making big bucks from this richest
and poorest of cities
but galloping buses are not pedestrians
to be tamed with words and money and this rare
soon to be extinct
what could have more impact than a bus bus
with a bellyful of passengers and its fluorescent plastic strip
sped past the bright shops and dark taverns
along third avenue where once
the great sad eyed el roared
and rattled tenement windows
and this rare soon to be extinct
what could have more impact than a bus bus
right outside the seventy-sixth street flophouse
where nightly floppers staggered home
amid swinging staggering singles
in the very crosswalk where daily the ancient monsignor
damn near ran out of breath while we wondered
how long he had left how many months or minutes
until he could no longer hobble to safety
before the light turned and he would be caught
in the stampede of uptown traffic and be killed
while we watched like the crowd at calvary
and did nothing to save him
we would carry the guilt to our graves
we would suffer gruesome memories
we would sweat through grisly nightmares
but he died quietly in his sleep
and the angels carried him away

and we were just streetcorner losers
with time to kill
then one day this rare soon to be extinct
what could have more impact than a bus bus
caught in mid escape a white pigeon
white as a baptismal gown white as a stained
glass window dove on a sunny sunday morning
a rare aberration of the prolific pigeons
those fellow gray loiterers
whose droppings whitewashed the steeples
of the church that spiked its windowsills
and swept up wedding rice before the flock could partake
a rare white winged apparition
caught like any of us might have been
by this rare soon to be extinct
what could have more impact than a bus bus
and it fell wide eyed
its feathers drifting slowly
spiraling white and red onto the asphalt
ground down by car after car until
even the blood disappeared
and the flying spirit disintegrated into the busy world
outside the dive bar beneath the flophouse
that will die and be reborn
in a paradise of condominiums and upscale cafes
with no room for the congregation
the aged priest may have been trying to save
with no room for elevated trains
or bored teenage boys
there was prophecy and revelation and the promise
of eternity and we knew
we too might grow old someday
if we were that lucky

Author's Commentary: Initial Ideas and Inspiration

In order to generate revenue, the transit company in the city where I now live wraps the entire exterior of a bus in an advertisement. There was a time in New York when buses had a lighted strip running across the roof on which an advertisement could be placed. The message "What could have more impact than a bus" was a way of encouraging businesses to post a message. My buddies and I sometimes hung out at the corner of 76th and Third, and an old priest would slowly cross Third Avenue on his way for a night cap. And once I did see a bus smash a pigeon on Third Avenue. A sad sight.

Author's Notes: Revision and Retrospection

The basic content of the poem stayed the same between the early and final draft: the bus, the old priest, and the pigeon.

One major change involved elaborating on our reaction to the imagined death of the priest.

selected lines from the early version:

in the very lane where daily the old monseignor
damn near ran out of breath while we watched
and wagered how long he had left how many
months or minutes until he could no longer hobble
to safety before the light turned and he would splatter
beneath the flophouse which will die and rise
and become a condominium scattering
the congregation he may have been trying to save
but he died humbly in his sleep instead
and we were just streetcorner losers

from the final version:

in the very crosswalk where daily the ancient monsignor
damn near ran out of breath while we wondered

how long he had left how many months or minutes
until he could no longer hobble to safety
before the light turned and he would be caught
in the stampede of uptown traffic and be killed
while we watched like the crowd at calvary
and did nothing to save him
we would carry the guilt to our graves
we would suffer gruesome memories and grisly nightmares
but he died quietly in his sleep
and the angels carried him away
and we were just streetcorner losers
with time to kill

Another major change was to end the poem in a way that would draw it together:

selected lines from the end of the early version:

and it fell wide eyed and feathers drifting slowly
spiraling white and red upon the asphalt
ground down by car after car until
even the blood disappeared
and the flying spirit disintegrated into the busy world

from the final version:

spiraling white and red upon the asphalt
ground down by car after car until
even the blood disappeared
and the flying spirit disintegrated into the busy world
outside the dive bar beneath the flophouse
that will die and be reborn
in a paradise of condominiums and upscale cafes
with no room for the congregation
the aged priest may have been trying to save
or for elevated trains or bored teenaged boys
there was prophecy and revelation and the promise
of eternity and we knew
we too might grow old someday
if we were that lucky

plaza of the undented turtle

sirens
red lights
angry cops
the gold car speeds
down avenue
c and swerves
onto the sidewalk
through the plaza
scattering
the twelfth street midnight
beer drinkers and slams
head-on into the shell
of the beloved
cement turtle
while the skyline sparkles
postcard pretty
outside our window
ten stories above
as we watch this drama
just another city night
just another summer street
just another urban legend
seeking anonymity
reality entertains
when it happens to others and
the door flies open
the foot race begins
run driver run
from police
run police run
into the night
flow river flow
to the mysterious sea
who knows

how it ends
is there justice
on dark streets
red lights gather and vanish
gather and vanish
all life long
blood bleeds
bullets kill
the turtle
does not cry
the pontiac
has chosen to remain silent
then the impounding officer
starts the engine
it purrs it revs and it's off
to automobile prison
there is no reporter
asking the cop at the wheel
about inanimate
reincarnation
it really does
have a phoenix
painted on the hood
there is irony
to fulfill
tragedy
lust
love and laughter
babies will surface from the womb
to crawl to walk to climb
searching
for the ecstasy of heaven
now the undented turtle sleeps
beneath the electric hum

of the power plant which may
or may not explode
with a hiss and a fireball
and a boom like the big bang
as if the universe were created anew
on the lower east side
and we are lucky just to breathe
amid the smoke and the screams
and we are lucky to survive
the chaos of night
and the turtle waits for the warm sun
for the silly day for the children
to play like creatures
on the back
of the great
creator
god

Author's Commentary: Initial Ideas and Inspiration

My future in-laws lived in an apartment on the tenth floor of a high rise at Twelfth Street and Avenue C, just across the plaza from the Con Edison power plant. One night, about a month before the wedding date, I was looking out their window. I heard a loud PFFFT. Then I saw a huge fireball that seemed to be a block wide and that rose high into the sky. Then I heard a boom. The lights went out, and people ran screaming through the plaza. As Roseanne Roseannadanna said, "I thought I was going to die." But my future mother-in-law said, "That happens from time to time," and did not seem worried. I guess she was right.

Many years later, when I was in The Bronx visiting my mom, I heard that there was an explosion at a Con Ed plant. So I called my mother-in-law. It had happened again, and this time, since it was post 9/11, the police were evacuating her building. Momma and her old dog could not make it down the stairs, so they were allowed to stay in her apartment. A few years later, during Hurricane Sandy, the Con Ed plant had yet another explosion, and we watched the event on the internet. So there was truth in Momma's words. Though she has passed on, the Con Ed plant is still there.

Another time, while I was still dating my future wife, I watched from Momma's window as the police chased a car, a Pontiac Firebird; it cut through the plaza and smashed into the cement turtle. It was night, and no children were playing on the turtle. The driver got out and ran off. I do not know why the cops were chasing him, or if they caught him, but the car started right up for the officer. And the turtle was unscathed. Absolutely undented.

Author's Notes: Revision and Retrospection

After I completed the early draft, there were no major changes until I did the final edits for the book manuscript. Given how easy it is to access the internet, which was not the case when the poem was drafted, I was able to determine that the car was a Pontiac Firebird. That would explain the painting on the hood, which I refer to as a phoenix. These lines were added:

the pontiac
has chosen to remain silent
then the impounding officer
starts the engine
it purrs it revs and it's off
to automobile prison
there is no reporter
asking the cop at the wheel
about inanimate
reincarnation

The driver may have gotten away, but the image of the car getting arrested seems a nice lead in to "there is irony to fulfill."

avenue b, 14th street, looking south

there is a place when
there is a moment where
crossing the street
all the streetlights stretching south
and all the traffic lights
align in rows
that would converge but for
some distant building
and i think i must be
exactly in the middle
of the street but i know
the world is too crooked
for that

Author's Commentary: Initial Ideas and Inspiration

When I was dating my future wife, we often walked from the Union Square subway station to Avenue C. One night while we were crossing the street I happened to notice this visual effect. If you are there some night, give it a try. But watch our for the cars!

Author's Notes: Revision and Retrospection

It is short, simple, and I do not recall any editorial struggles after getting the initial wording onto the page. The poem was written in the 1980s. Positioning it after "plaza of the undented turtle" seemed appropriate: the two poems are set within a few blocks of each other.

the push and break and chase of it

three men push a broken car down the street.
a dog chases them.

three dogs push a broken man down the street.
a car chases them.

three cars push a broken dog down the street.
a man chases them.

three men, three cars, three dogs
push each other down the street,
chase each other,
break each other.

no, no, we must not upset the order,
said the car who was really three cars who had chased the dogs.

a little innovation is in order every now and then,
said the man who was really three men who had chased the cars.

do we not constitute a microcosm of the universal flux
from order to disorder to the establishment of a new order
to be set to chaos?
said the dog who was really three dogs who had chased the men
and who now chased cars
following a wholly new ordering
of ordinary
affairs.

Author's Commentary: Initial Ideas and Inspiration

I was working at my uncle's shoe shine parlor and saw a couple of guys pushing a car down Brook Avenue. A stray dog started to chase them. It was an image I could never forget. The style of the poem is influenced by Russell Edson.

Author's Notes: Revision and Retrospection

Once drafted, this poem did not require much editorial attention, although I did deliberate about whether or not to use punctuation. It is quirky, and a bit different in style from the poems that precede it, but the image of a dog chasing a broken car seemed appropriate to the book, and "a wholly new ordering of ordinary affairs" seemed to provide a suitable ending for the first section.

II

...our spirits drink immortal rage and compassion from the fluorescent green ooze of the waterbug writhing fountain of youth

the third avenue el

I. 1886

a bridge and shining rails span the river
the long arm of the el stretches north
from harlem through the mainland
the seeds of the bronx are sown
tenements will blossom on fertile ground
there will be streets and streetcars and immigrants

will brave the broad ocean for their chance
in the land of the free
the colossus rises above new york harbor
glorious timeless stoic
her mighty limb bears a beacon of hope
a wary welcome to the new world

where geronimo is imprisoned
where chinese laborers are expelled from seattle
where former slaves are massacred in a mississippi courthouse
no one is indicted for their murder
in this great republic where the lord
and manifest destiny work in mysterious ways

a torch a tablet a stern look
staring toward the tempestuous atlantic
the copper matron will guide
exiles to the promised land
sure footed she is stepping
in the direction of south ferry station

II. 1920

from the battery park aquarium
to the botanical gardens and beyond
all for a buffalo nickel
a stadium will be built and there will be baseball
in the bronx and babe ruth and the yankees
will come and the crowds will cheer

in the golden age when the poor
inherit the earth one apartment at a time
the multitudes have arrived a new world is rising
farms become tenements
immigrants become americans
who will rest who will eat who will work

who will raise families and ride that great train
to a modest job and home to a modest kitchen
commuters flicker past trackside windows
curtains flutter and the glass shakes
garlic and cabbage and old country recipes
simmer on the flames of freedom

green stanchions green stations
lady liberty has turned green above the gray water
the sidewalks are gray the tenements are brown
or white or gray or red and the street gets little sunlight
children play and laugh in the shadows
the el sparks and thunders and storms across the sky

III. 1955

the sons and daughters of immigrants
survived poverty and prohibition
the depression and two world wars
now their children are given dog tags
and schools teach to duck and cover
when atomic bombs explode

but the economy is booming
the city thrives and factories flourish
televisions toys cars
disneyland gunsmoke the mickey mouse club
mcdonald's opens in illinois and eisenhower
sends aid and advisors to vietnam

this humble train this noble artery of democracy
the bronx harlem yorkville
lenox hill murray hill
little italy and chinatown
in this land where liberty proudly enlightens the world
rosa parks is arrested and the boycott begins

the third avenue el is mortal it lives it moves
it dies a long slow death
the aquarium has been closed and the fish deported
ellis island is abandoned to rot in the harbor
on the final manhattan run people doff their hats
and toast the last echoes of its passing glory

IV. 1973

the once great el is merely
a minor shuttle an appendix
lost in the intestines of the bronx
the dodgers and giants have migrated west
the yankees wane and rust
mottles the rivets of industry

america the beautiful wrestles with itself
broken glass lost dreams
riots and assassinations
planned obsolescence and withdrawal with honor
the weary el clatters like a faithful milk wagon
while tenements crumble and die

the world trade center rises above the skyline
the last passenger run is made in the dark
and the train disappears in the night
the streets will be quiet and sidewalks
freed from shadow but the world
will not seem so wonderful

towers will rise where towers have fallen
the bronx will rise from the ruin
ellis island will reopen and the children
of the children of immigrants will come
to behold that great green lady
her colossal foot trampling forever the broken chain of slavery

her torch pointing to heaven
where stars are innumerable stations

and the great train rumbles toward paradise

Author's Commentary: Initial Ideas and Inspiration

My mother had fond memories of riding the Third Avenue El from the Bronx to the Battery Park Aquarium. I remember a slow ride through a decaying Bronx. And seeing a transit policeman lock the Bedford Park Station as the last section of the El was being closed. It was late at night; my girl friend and I had left the back entrance of Fordham University and were walking along Southern Boulevard. The midnight silence was broken by the clank of metal as the lock was placed on the gate. But the poem is not based on personal memories; it is the product of many hours of research. I found it fascinating that the rails crossed the Harlem River to The Bronx in the same year that the Statue of Liberty was dedicated. And that the World Trade Center was completed in the El's final year. The Third Avenue El opened The Bronx to development; it seemed fitting to tell its story in terms of American and Bronx history.

Author's Notes: Revision and Retrospection

The earlier version of the poem was not divided by years:

the third avenue el (2008)

I. the new colossus

liberty enlightening the world
a torch a book a stern look
glorious timeless stoic
staring toward the tempestuous atlantic
the great torch in the great harbor
flickers a wary welcome

this is the land of the free
like buffalo the indians vanish
by boatloads the americans arrive
the tired the poor the wretched
masses huddled on the teeming shores
of lower manhattan

the year of our lord 1886
the new colossus rises from the waters
the year of our lord 1886
the great aqueduct of humanity
bridges the harlem and trains rumble
to the bronx to the mainland to the paradise across the river

the third avenue el is mortal it lives it moves
and the great green lady has donned her robe
with a book to read and a light to guide
exiles to the promised land
sure footed she is stepping
in the direction of battery park terminal

II. the torch

rivet by rivet the rails move north
from the straight torso of manhattan steel tracks curve
a mighty arm of enlightenment betokening
the golden age of the beautiful bronx
where the poor inherit the earth
one apartment at a time

and the new world rises from fertile fields
bronx farms become bronx tenements
immigrants become bronx americans
who will rest who will eat who will work
who will raise families and save their nickels and ride
that great train to a modest job

and home to a modest kitchen
where old country recipes simmer
on the flame of freedom
the aroma of garlic and cabbage permeating
the airshafts while commuters flutter
past bedroom curtains and the windows rattle

green stanchions green stations
the sidewalks are gray the tenements are brown
and children fill the streets with games and laughter
the wheels squeal the third rail crackles

children who grow and fight in foreign wars
and look to heaven when thunder rumbles the rails

III. the book

influenza prohibition depression
war and more war
the pages of history are written in blood
and sweat and tears
children wear dogtags
children are taught to duck and cover

when the bombs strike and children
watch cranes remove the main line
from the bronx hub to battery park
the aquarium has been drained
ellis island is closed and the great statue watches
for ships which do not come

the once great el is merely
a minor shuttle an appendix
lost in the intestines of the bronx
the dodgers and giants migrate west
the yankees wane and rust
mottles the rivets of industry

america the beautiful wrestles with itself
riots and assassinations
planned obsolescence and withdrawal with honor
on rotting ties and flattening rails the weary el
clatters like a faithful milk wagon
the tenements crumble and die

IV. the eternal flame

the last run is made in the dark
near midnight the motorman waits
the policeman padlocks each station
the train whispers through the darkness
to whatever land of forgotten dreams
trains go to when they die

broken glass shattered tenements
and the bronx burns
cranes uproot ancient steel
third avenue is open to the grim sunlight
the sidewalks are no longer in shadow but somehow
the world is not so wonderful

urban decay and suburban sprawl
the bricks lie where they have fallen
the statue stands above the gray water
exodus and crime
bankruptcy and terrorism
this is the valley of the shadow of death

where the el no longer runs
and there is love amid the ruins
the bronx is not dead
it is just being reborn
the great dream smolders in the wasteland
saplings and townhouses grow from the rubble

twin towers will rise where twin towers have fallen
above the gray waters above the gray city
the great torch of liberty points
to heaven where stars
are flickering stations
and the great train inches toward paradise

The metaphorical titles for the sections did not seem the best choice, so I decided to use four significant years as the controlling structure: 1886, when the railroad first crossed into The Bronx; 1920, when the El reached its northernmost point at Gun Hill Road; 1955, the closing of the line south of 149th Street; and 1973, the last year of service. This approach helped focus the poem; it allowed for clearer connections between the El and the Statue of Liberty while touching on United States and Bronx history.

I spent hours on the internet doing research. I took a video train ride through The Bronx, through pristine neighborhoods that years later would show the signs of devastation.

I heard recordings of its deafening roar. There is something to be said for underground rails.

And I read about the Statue of Liberty.

I spent a lot of time trying to find photographs depicting the color of the El's stanchions. I really wanted them to be green, as I was making a comparison to the patina on the Statue of Liberty. Most of the photos were black and white, and the color photos left much to be desired in their quality. I even contacted a transit historian.

Finally, I looked at catalogues from paint suppliers. I found one color, olive green, which was a brownish green, but it had green in the title. Not the green of the Statue of Liberty, but it was called green, so I went with the lines: "green stanchions green stations / lady liberty has turned green above the gray water."

According to an article by the Library of Congress, an early model of the Statue showed a broken chain and shackle in her left hand. This image of the end of slavery was replaced by the book, and was relocated under her foot; it is not very visible from ground level.

In other sources I read about the Carrollton Massacre and the Seattle Riots which occurred in 1886, the year of the Statue's opening. These events were sad, tragic, ironic. And representative of a country that had not lived up to its ideals.

I had a great wrestling match with the third stanza of the first section. In 1886, the Supreme Court accepted the idea that corporations are entitled to equal protection under the law. What a cruel contrast to the actual treatment of Native Americans, Chinese Americans, and Black Americans.

This version of the stanza reflected that contrast:

selected lines from "the third avenue el" working draft

in the land of the free where neither man
nor corporation may be denied
"equal protection of the laws"
and geronimo is imprisoned and chinese laborers
are expelled from seattle and former slaves
are massacred in a mississippi courthouse

After many hours this final version evolved:

selected lines from "the third avenue el" final draft

where geronimo is imprisoned
where chinese laborers are expelled from seattle
where former slaves are massacred in a mississippi courthouse
no one is indicted for their murder
in this great republic where the lord
and manifest destiny work in mysterious ways

Given the influx of immigrants into New York Harbor, and the poem by Emma Lazarus, the Statue of Liberty became increasingly associated with the immigrant experience, and not with freedom from slavery. My grandparents were immigrants, and this poem, as well as "welcome to mainland," reflect the promise of hope that they believed America offered.

I was also concerned that this poem, "the third avenue el," would not duplicate images from "welcome to the mainland." I worked on the two poems during the same general time period, and I think I succeeded in keeping them distinct.

standing upon the fordham road bridge

on a walk from nothing to do to nowhere to go
i stop here beneath heaven and above the harlem
river which curves from spuyten duyvil to hell gate
past the train yard and bus barn and power plant
through bluffs of tenement and project
in a valley veiled in concrete and night

all those little people with their big lives
all those big people with their little lives
asleep now or wandering the streets
searching for a cool breeze in the humid gloom
or cheap or expensive thrills which bring
forgetfulness of whatever pain there is to life

and i have found the river
darker and deeper it seems than space itself
though the sky is a gray haze of city light
which obscures the stars as we are obscured
and i stand above unheard currents
where tall masted ships no longer sail

i watch striations of light on the midnight water
which casts no human reflection
and tells no tales of what it carries away
the silent inscrutable current is a thirst
to be salted by unfathomable oceans
and in the depth of this drowning darkness

the faint vision of dawn
bringing a new day to this weary world

Author's Commentary: Initial Ideas and Inspiration

I remember walking across the bridge with a friend; we wanted to see an oldies band at a bar in Inwood. But the show was sold out. Bummer.

On our return trip, we stopped on our walk and looked down at the river.

Sometimes a poem springs from the memory of a mere moment.

Author's Notes: Revision and Retrospection

I found this draft in one of my notebooks:

standing on the fordham road bridge (1988)

on a walk from nothing to do to nowhere to go
i stop somewhere between heaven
and the harlem river which runs
like a neverending subway from spuyten duyvil
to the hellgate
beneath bluffs of tenement and project
all those little people with their big lives
all those big people with their little lives
asleep now or wandering the streets
searching for a cool breeze on a humid night
or cheap or expensive thrills which will
bring momentary forgetfulness to whatever
pain there is to life
searching for a sweet dream
the river is darker and deeper it seems than space
itself though the night sky is a grayish pink
a hazy reflection of city lights which obscure
the stars like we are obscured
we cast no reflection
striations of light on the midnight water
a thirst to be salted by the unfathomable oceans
of souls and molecules which have gone down the river

This is the 1995 version that appeared in *North Coast Review:*

standing upon the fordham road bridge (1995)

on a walk from nothing to do to nowhere to go
i stop somewhere between heaven
and the harlem river which curves
dark and shiny like a neverending subway
from spuyten duyvil to the hellgate
past train yards and busbarns and power plants
beneath bluffs of tenement and project
through a valley veiled in concrete and night

all those little people with their big lives
all those big people with their little lives
asleep now or wandering the streets
searching for a cool breeze on a humid night
or cheap or expensive thrills which bring
momentary forgetfulness of whatever
pain there is to life
searching for a sweet dream

and i have found the river
waters darker and deeper it seems than space
itself though the night sky is a grayish pink
a haze of city lights which obscure
the stars as we are obscured
and i stand above the unheard currents
hum of tired tire on the rusted plates of the drawbridge
at the halfway point between the two towers

awaiting the ship which does not sail
and i watch striations of light on the midnight water
which casts no human reflection
and tells no tales of what it carries away
souls and silt and civilization's sewage
the silent inscrutable current which is
a thirst to be salted by the unfathomable oceans

and i walk off up the great hill
while litter blows like pollen in the dawn breeze

This poem is really about the University Heights Bridge, which, mistakenly, I had always called the Fordham Road Bridge, because it enters The Bronx at West Fordham Road.

It is the experience of being in the city, surrounded by the city, and yet of being somewhere else, in the sky, above the water. And at night the city lights reflect on the currents, and the river keeps flowing in a dark and haunting way.

The 1995 version was written in three stanzas of eight lines, followed by a seven line stanza with a two line finale. I changed this to four six-line stanzas with a two line finale. This allowed the poem to fit on a single page, and that helped my overall layout.

I prefer to start two-page poems on the left page (verso) so that the reader can see that they are continued on the right (recto). I needed a one-page poem, and this piece seemed a good choice to follow "the third avenue el."

Keeping the poem on a single page also keeps printing costs down. A practical motivation, but I do think this poem benefited from the pruning and revision.

(The reader will notice that I have not been able to apply the start-a-two-page-poem-on-the-left rule to this *Annotated Edition;* it just would not work.)

The revised ending echoes Hamlet's lines: "How weary, stale, flat, and unprofitable / Seem to me all the uses of this world." But it also offers a bit of hope: "the faint vision of dawn / bringing a new day to this weary world."

A better ending, I think, than "litter blowing in the breeze."

halloween

detroit burns and the bronx is mugged
with socks full of stones the wicked beat
money from mortal flesh
pirates and devils
torment candy from the naive

riots and thievery and war always war
there are no loving arms
strong enough to fend off the world
blood and grief and bloated bodies
children starve and the innocent die but tonight

the slaughtered will rise from sprawling graves
tonight urchins will drift across mine fields
their ghostly songs whine like artillery
and in mockery eggs splatter
like bombs from unseen rooftops

o do wear a mask of a monster or mutant
it is less hideous than to look
helpless into the face of humanity
there were saints and gods among us
and we killed them

blessed are the dead who have been purged
of cruelty and greed
they know what we have lost
forlorn paradise heaven uncreated
they know and they will come

the intentionally killed the merely neglected
they who should fear but who love nevertheless
they will come who have been liberated
from the perpetual procreation of pain and stolen joy
they will come and they will dance

look look their bliss wafts through the tangible
we smile and we pray that the children will be safe
let us feed the darling monsters coin and corn
we who are so generous and who will send yet more
souls suffering to their graves for our great blessing

Author's Commentary: Initial Ideas and Inspiration

It is difficult to look at the dark side of humanity, at the pain and suffering caused by war, genocide, and violence. The early version of the poem recalls arson in Detroit, stores on Fordham Road closing early to avoid being robbed by people wearing masks, and the Rwandan Genocide. Halloween may have had its roots in the belief by some cultures that this is a time of the year when spirits could enter the world of the living or when souls could emerge from their graves. I play with the idea that souls of the dead will reappear, and that we will treat the trick-or-treaters while continuing our violence.

Author's Notes: Revision and Retrospection

These are two earlier versions:

halloween (early 1990s)

tonight we may see the dead
only the living will hurt you
my parents said and they did
there are no living loving arms
strong enough to fend off the world
the riots of summer
the winter shadows where thieves lurk
and the war always the war
politics and heroism
young blood and old grief

bloated bodies beside the river
the children the innocent die
tonight soldiers will rise from sprawling graves
tonight urchins will drift across the minefields
their ghostly songs whining like artillery
while eggs drop like bombs from the rooftop
detroit burns the bronx is mugged
police pummel whom they may
and throw carcasses to angry lawyers
pirates and devils torment
candy from the naive
the apples are poisoned and the princess
hopelessly lost
with socks full of rocks the learned beat
money from mortal flesh
o do wear a mask of a monster or mutant
it is less hideous than to look
helpless into the face of humanity
there were saints and gods among us
and we killed them
blessed are the dead who have been purged
of cruelty and greed
they know what has been lost
forlorn paradise heaven uncreated
the perpetual procreation of pain and stolen joy
our fathers and fetuses
Ghandi and Buddha
Christ and the Great Earth Mother
the intentionally killed the merely neglected
they who should fear but who love nevertheless
they will come who have been liberated
from pride and rage
they will come and they will dance
look look their bliss wafts through the tangible
we smile and we pray that the children will be safe
let us feed the darling monsters coin and corn
we who send yet more
suffering to their graves for our great blessing

halloween (2008)

tonight we may see the dead
only the living will hurt you
people say and they did
there are no loving arms
strong enough to fend off the world

pirates and devils
torment candy from the naive
detroit burns and the bronx is mugged
with socks full of stones the wicked beat
money from mortal flesh

summers of riot
winters of shadow where thieves lurk
and war always a war
blood and grief and bloated bodies
children starve and the innocent die but tonight

the slaughtered rise from sprawling graves
tonight urchins drift across mine fields
their ghostly songs whine like artillery
and in mockery eggs splatter
like bombs from unseen rooftops

o do wear a mask of a monster or mutant
it is less hideous than to look
helpless into the face of humanity
there were saints and gods among us
and we killed them

blessed are the dead who have been purged
of cruelty and greed
they know what we have lost
forlorn paradise heaven uncreated
they know and they will come

the intentionally killed the merely neglected
they who should fear but who love nevertheless
they will come who have been liberated

from the perpetual procreation of pain and stolen joy
they will come and they will dance

look look their bliss wafts through the tangible
we smile and we pray that the children will be safe
let us feed the darling monsters coin and corn
we who who are so generous and who will send yet more
souls suffering to their graves for our great blessing

From the 2008 version to the 2016 final, the last five stanzas were unchanged. The opening was transformed, and the first three stanzas were condensed into two.

The final 2016 version begins with "detroit burns and the bronx is mugged." It is reprinted here to make it easier to compare with the 2008 version:

beginning of the final version:

detroit burns and the bronx is mugged
with socks full of stones the wicked beat
money from mortal flesh
pirates and devils
torment candy from the naive

riots and thievery and war always war
there are no loving arms
strong enough to fend off the world
blood and grief and bloated bodies
children starve and the innocent die but tonight . . .

ne cede malis: **poem for the seal of the borough of the bronx**

yield not to evil
meet misfortune boldly
wings spread
head cocked
beak in profile
one stern
alert eye
stares forth
the bald eagle is perched
atop the hemisphere
the stylized cupule
of an acorn
a triangular shield
where the sky is broken
by the straight beams
of a circular sun
whose indifferent eyes
surface over calm water
peace and liberty shining
on the ripples of commerce
and at the base
a small triangle
dark
almost insignificant
it is the land
of new hope and old tradition
behold it is the bronx
here unseen millions create their lives
and await their fate
in the scroll
the ominous motto
ne cede malis
yield not to evil
all is surrounded

by a festooned circle
a suggestion of universal harmony
the sun has eyebrows
it is all so placid
the sky is cloudless
the waters still
the land a mere shoreline
a speck in eternity
and the eagle
watches his back
a wary carnivore
in a troublesome world

Author's Commentary: Initial Ideas and Inspiration

This poem has a unique subject: the Seal of The Borough of the Bronx. Where else could it get published, but in a book of poetry about The Bronx? I was most pleased that it also did find a home in the 2008 *Bronx County Historical Society Journal.* But for the Historical Society, I might never have come across the Seal, nor learned about its symbolism. The image that inspired the poem appeared in *BCHSJ* in the 1990s. It was black and white, with no color to distract from its starkness. Peace. liberty, commerce, and hope are represented by the sun and the eagle. To me, the sun looked so indifferent, and motto, "yield not to evil," seemed so fascinating. I could not resist writing about it.

Author's Notes: Revision and Retrospection

The 1991 version was written based upon a black and white image. The color version of the Seal, now available on the internet, is not as ominous as its black and white counterpart. I wonder what the poem would have been like if I had viewed the color version first. Be it as it may, The Bronx of my youth was not a paradise. This is reflected in a very rough first draft of the poem from a 1991 notebook:

***ne cede malis* early draft (1991)**

ne cede malis the motto
yield not to evil meet misfortune boldly
the bronx flag flies over the bronx
well maybe outside some municipal building
its sun has indifferent eyes and shines
inside an acorn beneath an eagle
is this symbolism or prophecy
i have seen pigeons fly
over the hollow eyes of arsoned tenements
the smell of smoke and decay
emanating from the doorway
buildings die like trees
stand dead for years
smell of smoke and decay
in this nut of reality

The challenge of developing this poem was to accurately convey the visual image of the Seal, as well as the meaning of its imagery. The final version is very different from the initial draft. But the last four lines: "and the eagle / watches its back / a wary carnivore / in a troublesome world" seem to keep some of the original sentiment.

washington comes to visit

he arrives at grandma's house
just off cypress avenue
but nana does not serve him a bowl of her soup
and poppop does not offer him a hand-rolled cigar
and dad does not take his picture
because they are not home
it is 1781 and even their home is not there
but the british are
and washington is scouting enemy positions
so the redcoats welcome him
with cannon fire
from harlem and randall's island and nearby ships
but the general
continues his visit and goes
to the shoe shine parlor on brook avenue
uncle al does not give him a free shine
mom and aunt jean are not standing in the doorway
aunt helen is not watching from her window
and grandfather does not run out
into 138th street as he does
to welcome roosevelt's motorcade
he shines the cops' shoes
so they let him shake
the hand of the beloved f.d.r.
but washington is not yet president
and the shoe shine parlor and 138th street
and cypress avenue and brook avenue are not there
though the millbrook is and so is the mill
and muskets fire and cannons roar
it is noisy as the fourth of july
and washington plans to attack manhattan
and bring peace and quiet to the neighborhood
but he marches to yorktown instead
and the rest is history

Author's Commentary: Initial Ideas and Inspiration

In the Spring 2002 *Bronx County Historical Journal,* Professor Lloyd Ultan gives an account of The Grand Reconnaissance. It is hard to imagine a Bronx landscape without tenements. In 1781, the British had a line-of-sight that allowed them to fire artillery from Harlem into The Bronx. According to Ultan, Washington arrived on the hill (140th Street and Cypress Avenue) as the shooting began. At one point, he was conversing with Rochambeau near the mill (137th Street and Brook Avenue) amid musket and cannon fire.

My father's family lived at 141st Street, just off Cypress Avenue, and my mother's family had a shoe shine parlor on Brook Avenue, not far from where the mill once stood.

On July 11, 1936, the Triborough Bridge opened, and Roosevelt's motorcade drove through 138th Street. According to my mother, her father ran out and shook the President's hand. The police let him do it. They knew him because he had shined their shoes. It may have been the best tip he ever received.

I have seen a photograph of Roosevelt's second motorcade on 138th Street (October 28, 1940). It was published in *Bronx Accent: A Literary and Pictorial History of The Bronx,* and also in *The Beautiful Bronx 1920-1950*. In the lower right, my mother and her sister can be seen standing in the doorway of 514 East 138th Street. Above them another aunt is looking out her front window.

Were he alive at that time, I am sure my grandfather would have run out again to greet his beloved President!

Author's Notes: Revision and Retrospection

I wanted to write a poem about Washington visiting the South Bronx. The original idea was along the lines of "even Washington fled from here."

This is from my 1991-1992 notebook:

washington fled

washington fled
amid fear
maybe landings at port morris
maybe men of war
sailing the shallow bronx river
three ambushes
route the hessians at pelham bay
each slaughter they thought the last
imagination exceeds reality
in this land of battle
who would be surrounded
on a peninsula
there's white plains
and new jersey
the suburban wilderness

This word-processing file is dated July 29, 1997:

washington fled here (July, 1997)

even washington retreated north amid fear
maybe landings at port morris
maybe men of war sailing up the bronx river
who wants to die on a peninsula
and the land was left to cowboys and skinners
political gangs who stole livestock of any persuasion

while the british fortified randall's island
to stare at the mainland
and they stared so long that the opposing sentinels
agreed not to shoot except for a rookie lieutenant
who was reprimanded and the practical peace prevailed
while the cowboys and skinners professed politics
but did not argue ideology with the cattle and horses they stole
and plundered the bronx
as the dutch had counterfeited indian currency

making sewant of imported glass
using glass imitations of the sewant
they hung a quaker three times here
leaving him penniless and almost dead
ne cede malis on the bronx flag
yield not to evil meet misfortune boldly
the sun has eyes and shines
inside an acorn beneath an eagle

having left the beautiful bronx manor
valleyed between rolling bluffs and blue estuaries
fruits were grown here and exotic trees collected
a mill was built upon the brook that became an avenue
and the orchards and the exotic trees
and the forest vanished beneath the buildings
the brook into a vast sewer

Much of the historical information comes from an old book, *The History of The Bronx and Its People.*

The Dutch did counterfeit wampum. That fact made it into a draft of "randall's island," then was cut as that poem was revised. It is alluded to in "p.s. 43" in the lines: "is that real money or are these guys just / a couple of broke tulip farmers with counterfeit wampum."

The reference to The Bronx motto and flag became the subject of "*ne cede malis:* poem for the seal of the borough of the bronx." The brook being subsumed by a sewer is referred to in "liberation: the brook avenue parking meter quartet."

In the summer of 2015, I was working to complete *from the banks of brook avenue* and to get the manuscript published. The idea of a poem about Washington had been on my list of possibilities for many years. Ultan's article about Washington's scouting expedition to The Bronx was a great resource, especially because of the specific details, and places, it mentioned.

At one point Washington's guides took shelter behind the mill at 137th and Brook Avenue. Washington and Rochambeau, amid the bombardment, had passed the hiding guards. So he really did visit the old neighborhood. But my family was not there yet.

I started to play with the idea of their not being there. This approach was much more positive than that of my earlier notes. I had fun imagining all the things that did not happen because my family was not there yet.

And I enjoyed suggesting that his plan to conquer Manhattan was motivated by a desire for quietude: "and washington plans to attack manhattan / to stop the noise / but he marches to yorktown instead / and the rest is history."

I was delighted to come up with that ending: historical accuracy, some speculation, and a corny joke.

grandfather: a photograph

standing outside
the shoe shine parlor
a short man
in a long apron
brushes in hand
elbows bent
a gray face
an impatient smile
as if to say
hurry
take the picture
there is work to do
my customers are waiting

Author's Commentary: Initial Ideas and Inspiration

In the shoe shine parlor, the one with the least seniority worked in the middle spot. I got a good view of the photographs in the long rectangular frame just above the bench. One photograph depicted my grandfather, aunt, and several uncles and customers. I used it on the cover of *the shoe shine parlor poems et al.* As I look at it again, my grandfather was not wearing an apron, nor were his elbows bent. But that is the image of him that I had in my head when I wrote the poem. In a way, this poem is a photograph of sorts.

Author's Notes: Revision and Retrospection

I think the poem makes a nice transition from "washington comes to visit" to "bootblacks on the loose." I did make some changes to it in 2015.

This is the original version that was published by *The Spirit That Moves Us* in 1981:

grandfather: a photograph (1981)

standing outside
the shoe shine parlor

a little man
in a long apron

brushes in hand
elbows crooked
& a gray face which says

hurry
take the picture
i have a customer waiting

bootblacks on the loose

we are bootblacks on the loose
and we might be found
in jersey or north of the county line
on summer tuesdays we swim
at palisades amusement park
the world's largest salt water pool
we cling to the board beneath the waterfall
and lose ourselves in the briny roar
saturday night it's pepper steak
at a chinese restaurant in yonkers
or a burger at ho jo's
where uncle al tries to convince
the waitress that i am an unusually short thirty-one year old
looking for a date
thought i am thirteen and still wrestling with puberty
sunday afternoon it might be
the bowling alley by yankee stadium
or the billiard parlor on brook avenue
cousin billy is gifted with great strength
and an abundance of enthusiasm
he subdues the pins with brute force
he breaks the rack with a thunderbolt
scaring the balls into pockets
and he pounds the leather into a shine
while sandy finesses his strikes and sweet talks
the bank shots and coaxes the shoes
to perfection
i suck at everything but have fun anyway
i am learning to sweat my way through a shine
not the strongest
not the suavest
but i get the job done
i cannot outswim
uncle al though billy

can beat him at bowling
and sandy can beat him at pool
but al's arms are like tree trunks
he has been a bootblack
longer than the three of us have been alive
and no pair of shoes
can make him sweat
he loves to take us places
when we are not working
and to play gin rummy when it rains
and to lie in the sun
on the boardwalk at palisades
and smoke a cigar after lunch
while we wait
so we won't get cramps
the proper amount of time
between eating and swimming
is exactly how long it takes
for al to finish his cigar
so we watch the manhattan skyline
and boats on the hudson river
and women in bikinis
and we wish
the day would never end

Author's Commentary: Initial Ideas and Inspiration

I came up with the title years before I had most of the content. From the line "we are bootblacks on the loose," I was able to recall the memories that re-create an awkward, innocent, and fun time of my life.

Author's Notes: Revision and Retrospection

One approach to the writing process is to widely explore the general topic, then focus and edit the work later, so many of the lines from the early notes do not appear in the final draft.

bootblacks on the loose (notes from 1997—2000)

after the graveyard shift at the freight yard
he drives up in the pale blue mustang
rumor has it his number came in once
and honks to gather his nephews
real or honorary
whichever happen to be working for him
that summer
for a morning swim at the palisades
and we drive off
while the ghetto basks in the morning sun
and the hoodlums are sleeping and the cops are sluggish
and the old ladies walk to their groceries
to the italian deli to buy heroes
guinea sandwiches we insiders call them
then it's off to jersey
to the best pool i could ever imagine
salt water which does not burn the eyes
a waterfall pushing gentle waves
we are bootblacks on the loose
when we work we work
ten maybe twelve hours a day
bent over the shoes till our feet swell
our hands cramp and our sweat
drips into the shine but now
it's summer it's tuesday
the shop is closed and we
are going swimming
uncle al has finished the midnight shift
at the railroad express agency
he honks at the corner to collect his nephews
we buy sandwiches and we are off
to the world's largest saltwater pool

we are bootblacks on the loose

it is summer it is tuesday
the shanty is closed and we
swim above the hudson
the world's largest saltwater pool
palisades amusement park
it is morning
the rides are sleeping
the game wheels are not spinning
the perpetual music
of 77-wabc drowns in the waterfall
we cling to the ledge
the water pours over our heads
and down our backs
we are lost in the water
blinded by the water
immersed in the water
we might be sea creatures
lulled by mermaid song
to a world beyond desire
lost in a womb
of cool liquid sunlight
we are bootblacks on the loose
it is summer it is tuesday
we are kings of the deep
end of the pool
ten feet down the eardrums throb
we strain to touch absolute bottom
the chipped paint bottom
of the world's largest saltwater pool
we rush to surface
to breathe in a world
so deep the skin is clean
of work
here there are no shoes to shine
it is like chimney sweeps in blake's heaven

Eventually, the poem began to find a new direction:

we are bootblacks on the loose

anything is possible
saturday nights it's
chinese in yonkers
or ho jo's on bruckner
al tells the waitress
i'm a thirty two year old midget
and a big spender but she just
smiles at her wedding ring
i'm really thirteen
more interested in dessert
and being out with the big boys
after a twelve hour day
of pounding brushes on leather
sundays it's the pool hall
big bill hits the balls so hard
they dive in the pockets to get away from him
sandy coaxes them soft and sweet
they do what he wants
i always seem to be
behind the eight ball or to find
something awkward like a pair
of men's jockey shorts in the center pocket
and dream that someday
i will be good at something . . .

This the draft that most immediately preceded the final version:

bootblacks on the loose (6/26/15)

we are bootblacks on the loose
and we might be found
in jersey or north
of the county line
on summer tuesdays we are swimming
at palisades the world's largest
salt water pool and we cling

to the boards beneath the waterfall
and our troubles wash away
saturday nights its pepper steaks
at a chinese restaurant in yonkers
or a burger at ho jo's
where my uncle tries to convince
the waitress that i am a thirty one year old midget
thought i am thirteen and still wrestling with puberty
sunday afternoons it might be
the bowling alley by yankee stadium
or the pool hall on brook avenue
cousin billy throws the ball with the strength of a gorilla
and smashes the rack into the pockets
and pounds the shoes into a shine
sandy finesses his strikes and sweet talks
the bank shots and coaxes the shoes
to perfection
i seem to suck at everything but have fun anyway
and am learning to sweat my way
through a shine
not the strongest
not the suavest
but i get the job done
but i cannot outswim
uncle al though billy
can beat him at bowling
and sandy can beat him at pool
but al's arms are like tree trunks
and he has been shining shoes
longer than the three of us have been alive
and he loves to take us places
when we are not working

As I worked on the poem, I tweaked the line breaks and wording. For the final version, I wanted a more effective ending. I kept remembering our lunch breaks on the boardwalk, our view of Manhattan, and how wonderful it all seemed to be. Finally, the lines emerged.

al

his father was a bootblack
and he is a bootblack
shining shoes with graceful movements
a faint smile beneath his moustache
while big band music plays on the ancient radio

and when the brushes dance
over the leather he leans
slightly like a man
gently holding the waist of a woman
in a prohibition era ballroom

Author's Commentary: Initial Ideas and Inspiration

An artist at work. He worked fast, but never seemed to hurry. He worked hard, but never seemed to sweat, though I am sure he did. Sometimes on a summer afternoon he would stand outside and stretch out his arms so that the breeze blew through the sleeves of his tee shirt. When you shine shoes in hot weather you are going to sweat. But cool people do not seem to show it.

Author's Notes: Revision and Retrospection

To develop a poem, it helps to contemplate the memory or image that inspired it. Uncle Al seemed to have a slight smile as he was buffing the shoes with a rag. And there seemed to be a graceful aspect to his posture. He liked county music on the radio, but would put on AM rock for us youngsters. Maybe sometimes he listened to ballroom jazz. I am not exactly sure anymore: it has been fifty years. But the image seemed to fit the poem.

early notes: al's arms

al's arms are like tree trunks
muscular flexible
not a bodybuilder but a man
who lifts boxes all night
in the railyards then opens
the shoe shine parlor and works some more
as he handles the brushes
a faint smile appears beneath his moustache
a fast shine but he never hurries
he paces himself but his pace is
efficient with fifty years of bootblacking
when he shines the sides of the shoes
he leans slightly like a man
gently holding the waist of a woman
in a prohibition era ballroom

p.s. 43

jonas bronck elementary school
he settled in paradise
on the east bank of the harlem river
divinely guided to a virgin forest
of unlimited opportunity
that needed only an industrious hand
to make it the most beautiful
region in the world he claimed
but we grew up on streets without trees
and we gathered in the auditorium to watch
space flights on a black and white television
the stage had a mural
of the purchase of the bronx
guys in tight black suits and long white stockings
and some sachem outside a longhouse
the suits were not spandex
and the longhouse was not made
of barclay-barclite fiberglass panels
and just beyond the panorama
maybe some old lenape was saying
there goes the neighborhood
they are letting the whites in
they do not even speak the language
is that real money or are these guys just
a couple of broke tulip farmers with counterfeit wampum
when a launch was delayed we watched reruns
of *my little margie*
then it was back to the space race
because america must beat russia to the moon
so the commies would not invade the bronx
and we stockpiled tanks and troops in europe
and we saved the world for democracy
though we could not save the neighborhood
from drugs and crime

and in our kindergarten classroom
midnight vandals threw the teacher's coffee into the aquarium
the goldfish was floating belly up in the morning
no one talked us through our sadness and fear
it was a tough school
if you barfed in the cafeteria you had to clean it up yourself
which led to more barfing
you cleaned and barfed till you barfed no more
and there was nothing more to clean
then you went to class or went home
my mother had her own memories
of this educational institution
where teachers put clothes hangers
inside kids' shirts to encourage good posture
and criticized mom because her parents spoke italian
and not good english
so when they sent letters home in spanish
which neither she nor i could read
she shared her disgruntlement at the main office
but the next letter came again in spanish
and she returned again and again
she was quite good at expressing disgruntlement
in perfect bronx english
most of us were not bilingual but we were quick learners
in kindergarten we were not taught the alphabet
but the first grade teacher assumed we knew it
we learned this is the way life would always be
full of irony and incongruity and strange paintings
and of love and disgruntlement and rebellion
in third grade i became enamored
with a leopard skin coat
there was a redhead inside it
i don't remember her name
but what a coat

when they painted the doors pink
and put a DO NOT TOUCH sign on the wall
how could i resist
shoving my hat into the wet paint
they would not arrest me for it
they would not send me to the principal
the redhead would not be impressed
even my mother would not yell
at something so absurd
it was like the rich taking money from the poor
it was like going to the moon while the world was dying
it was like sending troops to vietnam
it was like arsonists burning tenements
even when the slumlords did not pay them
it was like writing poetry
instead of working on wall street
it was like jonas settling the bronx
and thinking he could improve paradise
it was because there was a sign
saying not to
it was because the tenements
were crumbling and the trees had vanished
and john wayne had killed all the indians
except for a few token sidekicks
it was because
it was there
and i had a hat
and the paint was wet
and i was a stupid kid
with a pink hat
receiving a great education
in america

Author's Commentary: Initial Ideas and Inspiration

One way to write a poem is to focus on an image, then write down everything that comes to mind about it. I attended P.S. 43 from kindergarten to third grade. The poem was written many years later, so it was a mental stretch to recall many of the specific details. But I remember lining up in the cafeteria to begin the day, the kid having to clean up after vomiting, and our vandalized kindergarten classroom. For years this poem remained on my "to do" list. My early notes for the poem were limited by my memories and by the printed materials I had read about The Bronx.

As I worked on the final version in 2015, the internet allowed me to research details that I may never have found elsewhere. The Barclay-Barclite sign loomed over the Major Deegen, but what was manufactured in that large building? Some sort of fiberglass panels, as far as I can tell. One of my aunts claimed that she went to school at P.S. 43 with Dutch Schultz, but I could not verify that, so I removed the reference from the poem. I checked to see when *My Little Margie* was originally broadcast; we must have seen the reruns.

The mural in the auditorium is still in my memory. I could not find a picture of it. I contacted the school and was told that there is no mural in the auditorium. I suspect it may have been a WPA project, but could not find it through my research, not even after contacting someone with expertise in that field. It is so sad that a part of Bronx history has vanished. I remember the mural as vividly as I remember the leopard skin coat. And the dead goldfish. And my mother's anger at the letters in Spanish. And leaving school with pink paint on my hat, and my uncle Al, the bootblack, restoring the hat with the benzene he used to clean brown shoes.

I paraphrased Jonas Bronck's comments about the virgin forest needing an industrious hand to make The Bronx the most beautiful region in the world, and I could not resist inventing the comment by the old Lenape. The Dutch really did counterfeit wampum. And at one point tulips were worth more than gold. According to what I read, the crash of the tulip market prompted the Dutch to expand their New Amsterdam colony.

Author's Notes: Revision and Retrospection

The early version was an expansive rant. It included references to the Webtech scandal, the savings and loan scandal, the Chrysler bailout, homelessness, health care, and economic inequality, as well as references to places such as the Mott Haven Canal, the coffee factory, the highway, the railroad, and the 600 school for juvenile delinquents. Most of these references were cut from the final version, but I think the final version retains the social commentary, perhaps with less anger and more humor.

I grew up in the same apartment that my mother did, and, from kindergarten to fourth grade, attended the same elementary school that she once attended. Her memories of a clean, safe Bronx contrasted the world in which I grew up.

When I use "street view" on the internet, I can see the old neighborhood, see the many new buildings or pocket parks that have been built on sites where tenements were abandoned or lost to arson. The devastation of the South Bronx was happening as America was investing in the space program and in the Vietnam War.

P.S. 43 is still standing. It seems that the schoolyard was renovated and reopened in 2017. Many years would pass, and many tenements fall to ruin, between my elementary school days and the rebuilding of the South Bronx.

My mother's anger at receiving letters in Spanish after her family had been belittled because the parents were native Italian speakers was part of our family lore. I included the story of her disgruntlement in the final poem; it does not appear in the 1998 draft.

The lines "when we ask for money for ice cream the fathers say / *do you think i'm rockefeller*" were deleted after the 1998 draft; they appear in a slightly different form in the poem "skully."

This early draft is much longer than the final version.

p.s. 43 (1998)

jonas bronck elementary school still stands
amid the ruins red and white above the rubble
of tenements where friends once lived
no one told us who he was or where
he settled in 1642 near the banks of the harlem
river beneath the barclay barclite sign that blinks
barclay
barclite
barclay barclite
on the square beamed industrial building
the past and the present are one
barclay
barclite
barclay barclite
in the waft of the coffee roaster
where the grand concourse and boulevard
butts the major deegan
the railroad crosses the river
broad streets carry crosstown traffic
the highways lead to new england and queens
the canal ran here long ago
i saw it once in a dream
as it may never have appeared
but history is illusion
what
was barclite
who was barclay
no one ever said or cared
it is as forgotten as the webtech scandal
so much for jobs in the south bronx
that's the south south bronx to you
the bronx that was

before the english arrived
right there on the mural behind the stage
in the auditorium where we assembled
to watch rocket launches
america had to beat the soviets to the moon
so the russians would not invade the bronx
and when there was a delay in the countdown
we watched *my little margie*
which made us laugh
the painting of the dutch guys
in strange clothes was not funny
spandex pants maybe and long stockings
but spandex was not invented yet
and well postured native americans
in loin clothes but we were too young
to know about loins
they were all making a deal
beneath the trees
as if there was a time before highways
this is the land the yankees made famous
and dutch schultz
money is heroic
sailing two thousand miles across the atlantic
is nothing
it was a tough school
if you barfed in the cafeteria
you had to clean it up yourself
which led to more barfing
you cleaned and barfed till you barfed no more
and there was nothing more to clean
then they called your mother
if you didn't behave there was
the 600 school across the street
with barred windows and fifty foot fences
it was delinquent land before there were too many
delinquents to school
they lied to us anyway
crime does pay
politicians and corporate executives
make more in a year than our fathers could in a lifetime
when we ask for money for ice cream the fathers say

do you think i'm rockefeller
what does the old man know
this was decades before reagan unleashed
the corporate wolves on the middle class
what is a corporation
but a being which cannot be hauled off to jail
chrysler or a savings and loan
can receive welfare but
wheelchair annie cannot
millions for defense but not a penny for youth
the right to life is the right to die in america
die in a war
die without a home
die without medical care
die in a crime
die in the electric chair
what the hell does anyone care
if you're not a fetus
you had your chance
they made you take it
the native americans could
simply say no to money
this land was so rich in wampum
that the jealous dutch counterfeited it
importing european glass
another economy broken by greed
money is a drug
like heroin but it's legal
and the law says
that little children must go to school
and i went
it was an old school
when my mother went there
a teacher put a clothes hanger
in a kid's shirt to promote good posture
they let us slouch if we wanted
as long as we wore shirts and ties
or skirts and dresses
it was where i learned
that in america you cannot go to the bathroom
when you want to

if you go in your pants
they make you sit in it
even if you are five years old
and that america
is the land of the free
as long as your definition of freedom
is like everyone else's
why should i believe in the moon
it is just another streetlight
without a pole
they made us collect leaves
and paint them
from whatever trees there were left
as if God's colors were not good enough
and we stood each morning
to pledge allegiance to the flag
and we had nuclear disaster drills
kneeling beneath our desks
but they did not allow us to pray
we lined up every morning
in military formations
they trained us
for war and work
if we did well they let us play
this was life as we knew it
there were film clips of eisenhower
talking to the soviets
and walter cronkite
took us to space
we were quick learners
in kindergarten we were not taught the alphabet
in the first grade the teacher assumed we had learned it
we knew this is the way
life would always be
in third grade i fell in love
with a leopard skin coat
a redhead inside it
i don't remember her name
but what a coat
they painted the halls pink
and put a do not touch sign on the walls

how could i
resist
shoving my hat into it
they would not arrest me for it
they would not send me to the principal
the redhead would not be impressed
even my mother would not yell
at something so stupid
it was like taking money from the poor
it was like going to the moon
it was like sending troops to die in asia
it was like arsonists burning tenements
even when the slumlords did not pay them
it was like writing poetry
instead of working on wall street
it was because there was a sign
saying not to
it was like the dutchman
settling the bronx
it was like dutch schultz
selling booze during prohibition
he went to school here too
in the good old days decades before
the drug dealers set up open air markets
it was because
the tenements were dying and the trees had vanished
and john wayne had killed all the indians
except for a few token sidekicks
it was because
it was there
and i had a hat
and the paint was wet
and i was a stupid kid
receiving a great education
in america

cypress avenue

the avenue is named for the trees
that once grew in the morris arboretum
before the age of development and ruin
they are gone but their spirits linger
on this quiet avenue in the noisy bronx
a half mile of peace and simple wonder
or is it just childhood illusion
the thrill of saint mary's park
the lure of the randall's island walkway
the corner candy store
that sells joyva halvah and joyva joys
chocolate covered raspberry jelly bars
so tart and sweet even hamlet
would find succulence in the dull world
at grandmother's apartment her cooking
brightens the railroad flat
the aroma seeps out the window
and the street seems to sparkle
there is a green beauty salon
a turquoise shoe shine parlor
p.s. 65 with its light brown bricks
sparrows chirp in the schoolyard
and when the basketball courts are deserted
in the solitude of a sunday afternoon
even a clumsy kid
can pretend to be an all-star
the millbrook housing projects
are young and pink
christmas lights blink in various windows
i watch the flashing colors
to the point of insanity
while daddy warms up his 54 plymouth
in an outdoor parking lot by a scraggly locust tree sapling
as the car radio plays

wonderland by night
and i wonder
about the abandoned public school
p.s. 29 is bone white in the harsh sun
a spectral glow in the dark
the children say it is haunted
and i am a child
and in a long narrow store
lost in the red and yellow flames
of arson perhaps
father buys me the black knight of nurnberg
it is the missing piece
of my collection of aurora plastic models
the red knight of vienna
the blue knight of milan
the silver knight of augsberg
there is a gold knight of nice
i do not know it exists but it would be nice to have
i would lust for it as i did for the black knight
but my temporal desires have been temporarily satisfied
i am happy for a while
and safe for a while
in bed at night surrounded
by stuffed animals that protect me from bad dreams
while the knights keep watch from my shelves
there are tears and joy
there are more things to fear in heaven and earth
than i can dream of
as i glue together the armor
that protects me from the world

Author's Commentary: Initial Ideas and Inspiration

According to my research, the street was named after the cypress trees in the Morris family arboretum. Cypress Avenue runs from the Triborough Bridge to Saint Mary's Park. For several years my father parked his car at a garage on Cypress and 137th Street, and I remember sitting in his Plymouth one night while he warmed it up. The radio was playing, and some of the windows of the Millbrook Projects were lined with Christmas lights. My grandmother lived just off Cypress Avenue on 141st Street. On the corner was a candy store, and across from that, P.S. 65 which had a large schoolyard.

Despite being lined with tenements, Cypress Avenue lingers in my memory as echoing with a sort of pastoral peace. Maybe the spirit of the trees emanates from the concrete.

Author's Notes: Revision and Retrospection

This is a meditation on a place. The early notes from 2000 ramble, but they do include the basic images which appear in the final draft: the abandoned school, sitting in the car, Christmas lights, and grandmother's house. When I worked on the final version in 2015, I walked the street on the internet. In my mind, I sat in that car again; I sat again in Nana's front room and tried to recall the view from the window. I could almost taste the jelly bars. And I remembered the Black Knight. I used the internet to ascertain the names of the other Aurora models in my collection, and I discovered the Gold Knight. I also came upon a photo of the abandoned school in its early days.

The original version of the final poem quoted two lines from Dee Clark's song "Raindrops." Just after receiving a manuscript proof from the printer, I learned that I would probably have to get permission to use the quote. I pulled the galley and reworked the poem.

I considered just referring to the title of the song, but I was afraid that readers might confuse it with "Raindrops Keep Falling On My Head." The B. J. Thomas song did not fit the mood of my memories, and it was not from the time period in which the poem was set.

So I mentioned Bert Kaemfert's "Wonderland By Night," which I also had heard on the radio while I was sitting in Dad's car. It was one of those rare occasions that I cherish: just being alone with Dad, sitting in the dark. Just us, doing nothing. It was wonderful.

Though initiated by my desire to avoid a copyright issue, the change from quoting from "Raindrops" to citing a song title turned out to be a fortunate one: mentioning "Wonderland By Night" carried over the images presented earlier in the poem, where Cypress Avenue is presented as a "quiet avenue in the noisy bronx / a half mile of peace and simple wonder."

I liked the flow from that song title to the lines that follow it: "as the car radio plays / *wonderland by night* / and i wonder / about the abandoned public school / p.s. 29 is bone white in the harsh sun / a spectral glow in the dark.

Most of the work on the poem was done in 2015.

These are some early notes:

cypress avenue notes (2000)

once the street was lined with american cypress
the morris family's arboretum
but i remember only the sumac in the parking lot
and the abandoned school that crumbled
beneath the housing projects
bone white in the stark sun
a gray shade beneath the moon
and i sat one night while dad warmed up the plymouth

staring into the windows
glimpses of christmas trees and blinking-light windows
the pink bricks of the high rises
new and baby pink
rise high on the horizon
they are the horizon beyond which there is nothing
but the rest of the world

the road to grandmother's house
is treeless and the wolves are watching
daddy wears a hat and trenchcoat
has flat feet and walks slow
they think he's a detective
mommy has a loud bark
the streets are full of deconstructionists
even philosophy has no meaning
the priests are praying
the mayor fiddles
while tenements burn . . .

skully

we squat we crawl we kneel
we lie on the sidewalk to shoot
bottle caps from square to square
in a game that demands
intimate contact with the street
and we play it with a summer frenzy
on a worn slab of cement outside 514
smooth almost as hallway marble
the only one like it on the block
in the neighborhood in the known world
unmarred by cracks and even
the residue of long discarded chewing gum
has become one with the surface
a man-made stone made perfect by time
and we study the board with the intensity
of pool hall hustlers and we flick
the middle finger off the thumb
make the shot and go again
hit an opponent and advance
we grow calluses on fingers and palms
we wear holes in dungarees years before
it becomes fashionable
our knees blacken but we do not care about arthritis
and we do not care how stiff the iron-on patches feel
before we wear holes in them too
our mothers mend and sew
our fathers say
who do you think i am rockefeller
when we ask for a dime to buy soda
so we do not ask for new pants
they were children of the great depression
they are hard working men and if there is change
in their pockets we will get that orange nehi
and we will save the cap and fill it

with melted crayons and we will line up
and shoot away the summer afternoon
angling from square to square
one to four on each corner
five through twelve midway on each side
thirteen in the center
again and again we crisscross deadman's zone
and must avoid disaster
like our fathers went from poverty to war to the thankless jobs
they are grateful to have
like the big boys flirt
with drugs police crime paternity
they hope to get out of adolescence alive
and survive their unknown futures
there is a wall around berlin
the russians are building missile bases in cuba
and vietnam looms beyond the sunset of many childhoods
the line between victory and defeat is chalk thin
we must make that crucial shot
into the thirteenth box
dead center in deadman's zone
and live to tell about it

Author's Commentary: Initial Ideas and Inspiration

In the days before the internet, I drew a diagram of the board in my notebook as best as I could recall. But how to describe the game to someone who did not grow up in a city? Now, however, a quick internet search reveals the playing area and delineates rules that I would have never remembered. I have not played skully in many years, and am now too old to crawl around on cement sidewalks.

The bottlecaps we used were the old fashioned ones that required a "church key," a bottle opener, to pry off, not the newfangled twist off caps. The delicatessens and supermarkets sold soda and beer in glass bottles, so there were plenty of bottlecaps around to use as game pieces or to nail onto the milkbox scooters we made.

I was playing skully, navigating box three, when I first learned that cats were resilient creatures. I heard a brief, but ever-loudening "rr-rooow." A cat that had fallen out of an upper story-window landed about a foot away from me. It got up and walked off. I considered putting this in the poem, but chose not to. Someday I may write a poem about the doppler effect.

Our favorite skully slab was just outside of 514 where my aunt lived. Her son, my cousin, was at sea during the Cuban Missile Crisis, so I left out the cat and chose the war theme, juxtaposing the deadman's zone of our childhood game with the real dangers of adulthood.

Author's Notes: Revision and Retrospection

Some kids referred to skully as "sidewalk checkers." My early notes tried to describe the game in detail. This became unnecessary because the rules of skully now can be found on Wikipedia.

These are some notes from which the poem emerged:

sidewalk checkers (2000)

bottlecaps and dungarees
poor man's golf
thirteen boxes
of all the street games this is the one
a street game where the players are one with the street
crawling on the sidewalk
aiming shots like pool players

thirteen boxes drawn on a cement square
four in the corners

five through twelve midway on each side
the numbers alternate across the board
shots six through eight
and ten through twelve
must cross the deadman's zone

to land there is to die
until another player hits your checker out
to collect the reward of advancing his piece
the offered number of boxes

players shoot from box to box
make the box and shoot again
miss and wait for the next turn
be spiteful and hit another player's piece
into deadman's land
or blast it off the board

thirteen boxes on a cement square
four in the corners
five through twelve midway on each side
thirteen in the middle
surrounded by deadman's zone

the numbers alternate across the board
shots six through eight
and ten through twelve
must cross the deadman's zone
to land there is to die . . .

This is a draft of the final poem:

skully (2015)

we shoot our bottlecaps from square to square
flirting with deadman's zone
we squat we crawl we kneel
we lie on the cement
like pool players aligning difficult shots

this big city game demands
intimate contact with the street
and we love it with a summer frenzy
that worn slab of cement outside 514
sea gray and smooth almost as hallway marble
the only one like it on the block
in the bronx in the known world
unmarred by cracks
even the residue of long lost chewing gum
has become one with the surface
this man made stone made perfect by time
and we shoot with thumb and middle finger
and we grow calluses on fingers and palms
and we wear holes in our dungarees years before
it becomes fashionable and our knees blacken with soot
but we do not care about arthritis
we do not care about how stiff
the iron on patches on the knees of our jeans are
before we wear holes in them too
and how our fathers say
who do you think i am rockefeller
when we ask for a dime to buy soda
we dare not mention ten bucks for new levis
they were children of the great depression
they are hard working men and if there is change
in their pockets we'll get that orange nehi
and cut down our pants to ragged legged shorts
and we'll save the cap and fill it
with melted crayons and we'll line up
at square one and shoot away
the summer afternoon
from square to square angling across deadman's zone
like our fathers went from poverty to war to thankless jobs
like the big boys flirt with
drugs police crime paternity
there is a wall around berlin
the russians are building missile silos in cuba
and vietnam waits beyond the sunset of many childhoods
the line between victory and defeat is chalk thin . . .

the tire man

nixon is rising and the yankees are falling
and i am walking to my political science class
i walk up the hill and down the hill
and a long way along fordham road
in my adolescent oblivion
and i stop
when a tire rolls across the sidewalk
i do not drive but i am a good pedestrian
i yield to rolling tires
even those not attached to cars
another tire follows it
and another
i see a tire lying on the ground
and the man in the back of a truck
drops a tire straight down so it hits
in just the right spot and rolls
across the sidewalk and up the ramp
to be caught and loaded onto the dock
they do not teach this in college so i watch
i cannot explain the vectors involved nor the probability
of repeatedly dropping a tire onto the exact spot
to give it sufficient momentum and an accurate path
i left the engineering program to become an english major
so the poetic beauty of it is enough for me
there are a few sliders and curves but the tires
always get to where they are going
and when the show is over i go to class
where tests are being returned and the professor says
i gave you 35 points for putting your name on the paper
because it is good to know your name
so how can one of you get a 42
i do not know who got the bad score
and i do not know the name
of the tire man

just another nondescript earning an honest living
he will never run for president
he will never pitch for the yankees
but there are no spitballs
and he throws a perfect game

Author's Commentary: Initial Ideas and Inspiration

Perhaps you can imagine my surprise at seeing the first tire roll by.

There really was a tire man, and I really did stop to watch, and the words of the professor are a pretty accurate quote.

The tire man had a simple job which he performed with great skill. Perhaps he is the urban, twentieth-century version of the common man the Romantics celebrated. Wordsworth was long dead, so I had to write the poem.

Author's Notes: Revision and Retrospection

The idea for the poem was listed in my notes, but I found no very early drafts. The poem emerged during the summer of 2015, when the manuscript evolved into a book with a tripartite structure. Initially, there were four poems listed in Section II. If I remember correctly, quick drafts of "washington comes to visit," "skully," and "cypress avenue" were added over the course of two weeks.

To get a sense of how the book was taking shape, I made a tentative layout using the 6x9 page size with the appropriate margins. I printed the pages back to back, with blank pages for poems yet to be written. It was a productive time for me; it seemed as if the manuscript, having taken some basic shape, had temporarily become a fill-in-the-blank project. Ideas that I seemed to have had for many years were now emerging into poems.

As part of this flurry, "the tire man," was written over the course of a few days. In my August 5, 2015 layout, there is a page with "tire man" in a text box to save the space. In the August 8, 2015 manuscript, the poem appears in almost final form.

The poem is set in the fall of 1971, when the Yankees had an 82-80 record and finished in fourth place, and Nixon was in the third year of his first term as president. I was glad to come up with the line "nixon is rising and the yankees are falling," as it seemed to justify the prosaic: "i walk up the hill and down the hill." The mundane moment is broken by the appearance of a tire on the sidewalk. After that the challenge was to describe the action briefly but clearly.

When I checked my college transcript, it seems that the professor's comment about test scores was actually made in the fall of 1970, in a political science class taught in the same building at the far end of campus that I was walking to when I encountered the tire man.

Perhaps because the image had been in my mind for so many years, the poem seemed to emerge quite readily. From first draft to the final edit, I changed the tense from past to present in these lines:

"tests have been returned and the professor says"
"there were no spitballs / and he threw a perfect game"

In the final edit, these lines:

"though the vectors involved and the probability
of repeatedly dropping the tire onto the exact spot
that gives it momentum and accurate path
can be explained but i left
the engineering program to become an english major
and the poetic beauty of it is enough for me"

become:

"i cannot explain the vectors involved nor the probability
of repeatedly dropping a tire onto the exact spot
to give it sufficient momentum and an accurate path
i left the engineering program to become an english major
so the poetic beauty of it is enough for me"

a small but perfect world

at thanksgiving we give thanks
for all we take for granted
the turkey the lasagne
the ceiling over our head
our apartment in the south bronx
the bedrooms are small
the dining room is not
we gather and feast
and the table is cleared
soon construction begins
the plywood is covered in a green grass mat
tracks are laid out and screwed down and wired up
engines and cars are placed on the rails for a test run
then the landscape is made complete
a city hall a bank a hospital
suburban townhouses
a farmhouse a barn and pens for the livestock
cows and pigs and chickens and trees
little people sitting on benches
at the station or on lounge chairs
at the little motel or in a suburban backyard
or walking to the diner or to the mailbox
or waving lanterns beside switch towers
there are platforms for the unloading
of milk cans and logs
a radar tower and a light tower
a water tank and crossing signals
these are the toys my parents never had
during the depression
now dad works in the financial district
where the buildings are tall and the streets are narrow
crowded by day and deserted by night
and before the world trade center
there are clearing houses and discount shops

so the bargains come home
the landscape is filled in
and expanded to the tall buffet
connected to the lowlands by mountains
which mom makes by painting grocery bags
and crumpling them and shaping them
a beautiful illusion in the heart of reality
a small but perfect world
where the streets are clean
and nobody gets mugged on the way to the store
where no one sets buildings on fire
or dies of an overdose in a back alley doorway
it is like living in the land of *leave it to beaver*
a small but perfect world
where there is much to be thankful for
christmas comes and the new year is celebrated
then each illusion is put back into its box
and the dining room table
is again just the dining room table
and school reopens
the cold of january sets in
and we are
still
thankful

Author's Commentary: Initial Ideas and Inspiration

With each passing year of my childhood the neighborhood continued on the road to despair. But within our apartment we celebrated the joys of life, of family, of Christmas, of the New Year. I was just a kid and did not understand the broader context, but my parents did: the Depression was over; the war years had ended; they were alive; the pantry was full; the rent was paid; there was money to raise a family, to buy a car, a television, and other goodies.

Lionel was in its heyday. In the dining room of our apartment in the South Bronx, we created an imaginary world where downtown streets were clean, where the suburban houses seemed comfortable, and where the farm was thriving with livestock and trees. Trains ran on time, except for the occasional derailment. It was fun. For me, a great childhood memory. For my parents, perhaps, a childhood they never had when they were young.

Author's Notes: Revision and Retrospection

The original notes were sketchy, and the original title suggested a focus on the plastic houses made by Bachmann. I had a pretty clear vision in my head of the track layout Dad usually used, and of where the accessories were usually placed. I did use the internet to refresh my memory, and I spent a bit of time looking at vintage Lionel and Plasticville products.

plasticville notes (7/28/15)

before the world trade center
there were clearing houses and discount stores
and my father worked on wall street
and the bargains came home . . .

the world is crumbling around us
and we think this is the best
of all possible worlds
we build a world of illusion while the tenements decay around us . . .

the fountain of youth

the sewer backed up and the street filled with glowing green water which all began when a neighborhood juvenile delinquent who was not very neighborly and who robbed from friend and foe alike like he just did not care lifted the manhole cover to show us the sights so we gathered to watch in awe brown walls of waterbugs writhing like times square on new year's eve and a few leapt up into daylight and into our nightmares for these were the winged tanks of the cockroach army whose armor mere sneakers could not destroy and we jumped back squealing and laughing then but not later and this neighborhood juvenile delinquent who was not very neighborly and who robbed from friend and foe alike like he just did not care liked to impress us so he threw seven milk crates perfectly suitable for sitting down the shaft but no one would sit in the street that hot summer night to talk and to watch the kids play punchball in the dark and there would be no open air games of dominoes or poker because the sewer backed up so much that the city sent a crew to repair it while we stood in the doorways to watch the strange sight of something actually getting fixed but things get worse before they get better the old timers always say and the maintenance crew flooded the sewer with dye which went down and came up and the waterbugs went down and the milk crates came up and the street filled with glowing green water which the maintenance men left like they just did not care so for a week no one played outside and the neighborhood juvenile delinquent hung out somewhere else and the shoppers and the commuters walked next to the buildings to avoid the chartreuse stench which took so long to recede that it became the evergreen symbol of what the city thought of us like it just did not care and of how we could not play on our own street which we would never forget though someday we might get lucky and hit the number or write a hit tune and move someplace where glowing green water would never happen somewhere like fifth avenue or sutton place where our bodies grow old and fat while our spirits drink immortal rage and compassion from the fluorescent green ooze of the waterbug writhing fountain of youth

Author's Commentary: Initial Ideas and Inspiration

The kid opened the cover, and the cylindrical wall of the manhole was crawling with waterbugs. Or at least what we called waterbugs. They were actually the American cockroach, a species which was not originally from America. They were large, about an inch and a half long. Though our tenements had plenty of German cockroaches, we seldom encountered the American variety indoors. But when we did, they were hard to kill. A sneaker stomp did not always work. A thick-soled Oxford was much more effective. So it was darkly exciting to view the writhing terror close up.

Why he threw the milk boxes into the sewer I do not know. Was this a premeditated plot to clog up the works, or just a spontaneous, goofy thing to do? Whatever it was, it did provide some momentary entertainment. But like many cheap thrills, the consequences were not fun. He could run wild and hang out on some other street, but our mothers did not let us around the corner, so we were stuck on our flooded, smelly block.

To call him a juvenile delinquent is a polite euphemism. He had often joined my cousins and the neighborhood kids in our childhood games, yet, as a teenager, he tried to steal from our family. He broke into my uncle's shoe shine parlor, but my uncle always took the money and quality brushes home every time he closed. And he also tried to break into my cousin's apartment by swinging down from a rope to kick in the bathroom window. As an English major, I think we may be touching on the theme of betrayal here.

But the ultimate betrayal was the city's failure to give its poor the same respect that it did its wealthy. A naive concept, but the poem is called "the fountain of youth." I worked in a church office on Manhattan's Upper East Side. The church was built over an underground stream. It had waterbugs. And rats. But no glowing green water would be allowed to stagnate on the clean streets of Manhattan's Silk Stocking District.

Author's Notes: Revision and Retrospection

An earlier version of this poem was published in *The Prose Poem: An International Journal.*

the fountain of youth (1993)

the sewer backed up and the street filled with glowing green water and it all began when a neighborhood juvenile delinquent who was not very neighborly who robbed from friend and foe alike like he just didn't care lifted the manhole cover to show us the sights and we gathered round to watch in awe brown walls of waterbugs writhing like times square on new year's eve a few leapt up into daylight armor plated waterbugs the winged panzers of the cockroach army that mere sneakers could not demolish and we jumped back squealing and laughing then but not later and he liked the attention so he threw seven milk crates perfectly suitable for sitting down the shaft just to impress us but no one would sit there that night because the sewer backed up when the crew came to repair it and we watched the strange sight of something actually getting fixed and the street filled with glowing green water which the maintenance crews left like they just didn't care so for a week no one played outside and the shoppers and the commuters walked next to the buildings to avoid the chartreuse stench which took so long to recede the evergreen symbol of what the city thought of us like they just didn't care and of how we could not play on our own street which we would never forget though someday we might get lucky and hit the number or write a hit tune and move someplace where glowing green water would never happen like fifth avenue or sutton place without losing the ripened dignity of the poverty of youth

III

...on the banks of brook avenue
where childhood is idyllic
and the world could not be more beautiful

welcome to the mainland

stagger from the atlantic's swell
seek land legs on ellis island
floundering through bureaucracy
and ferried to narrow streets awash
with humanity on the golden shores
of lower manhattan

the brooklyn bridge is a masterpiece
a magnificent temptation
but that alluring long island
stretches east and disintegrates
it points back to the world
you sailed so long to leave

now you migrate north
your ship has come and it has left
you tired and poor
yearning masses huddled and tossed
by the rattle and rock of the train
metal wheel upon metal rail

grinding and sparking
through the wonders of the city
beyond hell gate to paradise
where the tenements are young
where freedom is a peninsula
with heat and indoor plumbing

the brakes squeal the doors
to the new world open
welcome to the mainland welcome
to the bronx where all seems possible
here subways whoosh
underground and roar through the sky

there are rooms for rent
there is always room for one more
friend relative countryman
for one more lost soul
for one more exile
and the horizon fills with brick and glass

behind every silver window lies a dream
which may or may not be fulfilled
and in the cold snuggling of dark winter
or the wriggling of humid summer nights
babies are conceived and they are born
in america

this is not the land of your birth
though the native tongue remains
and the food tastes familiar
at dinner time that old world aroma
wafts through the hallway
the clatter of pots and pans

reverberates in the air shaft
where clotheslines sag with laundry
readied for the great
assimilation of work and school
backyard and alley echo
with multilingual profanity

prayers rise to the heavens
there are churches and synagogues
street corner preachers
rooms where idealists
contemplate utopia and the right
to believe or not to believe

there are times of prosperity
times of common despair
and always the children play
on sandlot and side street
in park and playground
they sing and cry and taunt and cheer

there are saloons and speakeasies
and saloons once again
ice cream parlors and candy stores
vaudeville and movies
all manner of entertainment
under the sun and under the moon

war will come and peace will come
again and again and there will be
parades and memorials and protests
you will grow old and remember
those days of struggle and joy
those friends relatives neighbors

lost in a changing world
where streets disappear and housing projects
spring forth like towers of babel
belgian blocks and trolley tracks
drown in rivers of asphalt
and moses parts the land

his great road cleaves its heart
there is exodus
poverty turmoil and tragedy
tenements burn and fall
there is rubble and more rubble
anger and desperation

ash and dust and broken bricks
and a spirit that suffers but does not die
and a hope that emerges
like weeds from the ruin
the survivors will fight
and new americans will come

the void will fill
with townhouses and pocket parks
there will be new music
new art and new words
and the aroma of exotic foods
will waft through the streets

fragrant and pungent
hopeful

and free

Author's Commentary: Initial Ideas and Inspiration

The Bronx is the only one of New York City's five boroughs that is not an island. The Third Avenue El, and later the rest of the subway system, gave immigrants the chance to escape overcrowded Manhattan. The newly built housing probably offered more comfort and more amenities than the tenements of lower Manhattan. I got a sense, from my parents, and from research, that The Bronx at one time was a poor man's paradise, or a workingman's paradise: the streets were clean, and people left their doors unlocked for the milkman or the ice man. For the better-off, there was the Grand Concourse. During my twenty years in The Bronx, I got to see its decline. After I left, things seemed to get worse. I see, from research, that there has been a resurrection. The rubble that I remember, the devastation that Mel Rosenthal photographed in his book *In the South Bronx of America,* seems to be no more. The Bronx has been rebuilt.

Though my personal experience has been one of loss, I try to give a sense of rebirth. Nevertheless, the feeling that has lingered in my gut for many decades is a naive one of tragic injustice: how could this be allowed to happen to begin with? In America? Perhaps the tragedy of The Bronx was a minor side-show in the grand drama of the Twentieth Century, with its world wars, regional wars, genocides, gulags, and cultural revolutions. But The Bronx was the slice of reality that I knew, and I know that its devastation should not have happened, not in an age when we have the technology and resources to provide for humanity—if we choose to do so.

I try in this poem to give a historical synopsis of the rise and fall and rebirth of the borough and to end on a positive note. Robert Moses remains an enigmatic figure. His Cross Bronx Expressway and social engineering, which often took the form of housing projects, destroyed many a Bronx neighborhood, and engendered ruination, but his parks and beaches brought delight, and the Triborough Bridge is a modern wonder.

Thematically, this poem is very related to "the third avenue el," and one of my tasks in editing the book was to make sure that the poems did not overlap.

Author's Notes: Revision and Retrospection

When I was young, I used a fountain pen to compose. I scribbled out notes, images, and rough ideas. When I had a poem to work on, or found a few lines that had potential, I printed them as neatly as possible. When I returned to the piece, I often recopied what I had already written before moving forward. This method has been replaced by the cutting and pasting on the computer. But the process of looking at the old before wrestling with the new continued. The computer makes it easy to rearrange words and refine line breaks, and to edit with a sense of how the poem will appear in print.

welcome to the mainland: early work on the opening (4-15-14)

stagger from the atlantic's swell
to seek land legs on ellis island
floundering
through bureaucracy
and ferried to the shores
of manhattan where the streets
are awash with people

the bridge is magnificent
a temptation indeed
but brooklyn is the beginning
of a long island that disappears
east into the broad ocean
pointing back to the world
you sailed so long to leave

the bridge is a masterpiece
a magnificent temptation
but brooklyn
leads to a long island that disappears
eastwards in the ocean
pointing back to the world
you sailed so long to leave . . .

welcome to the mainland opening (5-6-14)

stagger from the atlantic's swell
seek land legs on ellis island
floundering through bureaucracy
and ferried to narrow streets awash
with humanity on the golden shores
of lower manhattan

the brooklyn bridge is a masterpiece
a magnificent temptation
the lure of the long island
that stretches east and disintegrates
pointing back to the world
you sailed so long to leave

so you will migrate north
your ship has come and it has left
you tired and poor
yearning masses huddled and tossed
as the train rattles and rocks
through the wonders of the growing city . . .

welcome to the mainland
behold the bronx
that beautiful borough beyond the rivers
there are parks and side streets
where your children can play
freedom is a peninsula

just beyond the wrestling rivers
across harlem and beyond hell gate . . .

Here the first two stanzas have reached their final form:

welcome to the mainland (6-5-14)

stagger from the atlantic's swell
seek land legs on ellis island
floundering through bureaucracy
and ferried to narrow streets awash
with humanity on the golden shores
of lower manhattan

the brooklyn bridge is a masterpiece
a magnificent temptation
but that alluring long island
stretches east and disintegrates
it points back to the world
you sailed so long to leave

so you migrate north
your ship has come and it has left
you tired and poor
yearning masses huddled and tossed
through the wonders of the growing city
as the train rattles and rocks

metal wheels grind upon metal rails
freedom is a peninsula
beyond the wrestling rivers of hell gate
and you have arrived
the brakes squeal the doors
to the new world open

welcome to the mainland
welcome to the bronx
where all seems possible
here subways whoosh
underground and roar through the sky
tenements rise in their wake

there are rooms for rent
and there is always room for one more
friend relative countryman
for the entire world
and the horizon fills
with brick and glass

behind every silver window lies a dream
which may or may not be fulfilled
and in the cold snuggling of dark winter
or the wriggling of humid summer nights
babies are conceived
and they are born

in america
this is not the land of your birth
though the native tongue remains
and the food tastes familiar
at dinnertime that old world aroma
wafts through the hallways

and the clatter of pots and pans
reverberates in the airshafts
where clotheslines sag with laundry readied
for the great assimilation of work and school
and prayers and curses in many languages
echo and rise to the heavens

there are churches and synagogues
and streetcorner preachers
and rooms where idealists
contemplate utopia
and the right to believe
or to not believe

your children will play
in sandlots and side streets
and parks and playgrounds
there will be times of prosperity
with work for all
and times of common desperation

there will be saloons and speakeasies
and saloons once again
there will be vaudeville and movies
and all manner of entertainment
under the sun
and under the moon

and war will come and peace will come
again and again
and the cobblestones and the trolley tracks
will be paved over and neighborhoods razed
and the pink bricks
of housing projects will rise like towers of babel

and the tenements will burn
and crumble and fall
and tourists will come and gape at the ruins
and ellis island will fall to ruin and be restored
and the bronx will burn to rubble and beget
pocket parks and duplexes and housing developments . . .

welcome to the mainland (10-10-14)

stagger from the atlantic's swell
seek land legs on ellis island
floundering through bureaucracy
and ferried to narrow streets awash
with humanity on the golden shores
of lower manhattan

the brooklyn bridge is a masterpiece
a magnificent temptation
but that alluring long island
stretches east and disintegrates
it points back to the world
you sailed so long to leave

you migrate north
your ship has come and it has left
you tired and poor
yearning masses huddled and tossed
through the wonders of the growing city
as the train rattles and rocks

metal wheels grind upon metal rails
freedom is a peninsula
beyond the wrestling rivers of hell gate
and you have arrived
the brakes squeal the doors
to the new world open

welcome to the mainland
welcome to the bronx
where all seems possible
here subways whoosh
underground and roar through the sky
tenements rise in their wake

there are rooms for rent
and there is always room for one more
friend relative countryman
for the entire world

and the horizon fills
with brick and glass

behind every silver window lies a dream
which may or may not be fulfilled
and in the cold snuggling of dark winter
or the wriggling of humid summer nights
babies are conceived and they are born
in america

this is not the land of your birth
though the native tongue remains
and the food tastes familiar
at dinnertime that old world aroma
wafts through the hallways
and the clatter of pots and pans

reverberates in the airshafts
where clotheslines sag
with laundry readied for the great
assimilation of work and school
prayers and curses in many languages
echo and rise to the heavens

there are churches and synagogues
and streetcorner preachers
and rooms where idealists
contemplate utopia
and the right to believe
or to not believe

your children will play
in sandlots and side streets
and parks and playgrounds
there will be times of prosperity
with work for all
and times of common desperation

there will be saloons and speak easies
and saloons once again
ice cream parlors and candy stores
vaudeville and movies

all manner of entertainment
under the sun and under the moon

war will come and peace will come
again and again
and you will grow old and remember
those days of struggle and joy
those friends relatives neighbors
lost in a changing world

where streets disappear beneath
housing projects which rise
like towers of babel
belgian blocks and trolley tracks
drown in asphalt
and moses parts the land his great road

cleaves its heart
there will be exodus
poverty desolation and tragedy
tenements will burn and fall
there will rubble and more rubble
and anger and despair

and the years will pass
and hope will grow
like weeds in in the ruin
the survivors will fight
for their stake in paradise
and new americans will come

and the void will fill
with townhouses and pocket parks
and there will be new music
and new art and new words
and the aroma of exotic foods
will seep through the streets

and ellis island will be become a museum
and liberty will enlighten the world

In the October 28, 2017 draft, the poem is almost in its final form, so that version is not included here, except for these two stanzas which were revised before the final version.

This stanza:

reverberates in the airshafts
where clotheslines sag with laundry
readied for the great assimilation
of work and school and pronounced
in many languages curses echo
through backyards and alleys

was later revised as such:

reverberates in the air shaft
where clotheslines sag with laundry
readied for the great
assimilation of work and school
backyard and alley echo
with multilingual profanity

And this stanza:

there are times of prosperity
times of common despair
and always the children play
in sandlot and side street
park and playground
the sound of laughter and joy and tears

becomes:

there are times of prosperity
times of common despair
and always the children play
on sandlot and side street
in park and playground
they sing and cry and taunt and cheer

america's favorite pastime

and so it came to pass that the shortest kid in ninth grade was tired of the tallest kid in ninth grade not tired of the vertical difference but just tired of being pushed around so one bright sunny bronx morning the short kid came with a baseball bat and chased the tall kid around the schoolyard until the teachers took the bat and sent us all to class in this melting pot school where we did not quite fit the recipe so the bureaucracy batted us around and threw us curveballs like having us retake the reading test because our scores were too high and declaring 85 the passing grade and decimating our academically advanced class of those with hispanic surnames or dark skin but maybe this was still better than last year in that other school where gangs beat up anyone who was not violent like that quiet little spanish girl who ran crying and screaming down the hallway after the principal came into the classroom and announced the names of kids who were being kicked out of the program and being sent back to eighth grade in their respective ghetto schools but what did the principal care she was just a little girl from some other neighborhood and this is america this is social darwinism this is junior high school where only the strong survive like that short kid with the baseball bat that they took away but they could not stop him and after school he took out a baseball from his pocket and chased the tall kid all the way to the train station and is it not america's favorite pastime to watch big guys beating on little guys and little guys beating on big guys while spectators laugh and cheer glad they are not getting beat up and just hoping to survive

Author's Commentary: Initial Ideas and Inspiration

It really happened: the short kid chased the tall kid, before school with a baseball bat, and after school with a baseball. As one who was bullied by classmates, I thought it was so cool. And I still do. The account of the principal purging our class is also true. I thought her insensitive handling of the matter stunk. And I still do.

Our academically-advanced class spent grades seven and eight, which we completed in one year, in a junior high school where chaos reigned. It was a new school, and construction had not been completed by the beginning of the school year, so several months passed until we had full days of class. There was a fair amount of vandalism and violence. (I wrote about this in a poem called "logic," which appears *in concrete pastures of the beautiful bronx*.)

In ninth grade, our class was moved to a junior high school in a different neighborhood, but it was obvious that we were not welcome. The term "bureaucratic malice" comes to mind.

Author's Notes: Revision and Retrospection

This earlier version is longer than the final; it gives more background about my two miserable years in junior high school.

america's favorite pastime (8/23/03)

and so it came to pass that the shortest kid in ninth grade was tired of the tallest kid in ninth grade not tired of the vertical difference but just damn tired of being pushed around so one bright sunny bronx schoolyard morning the short kid came with a baseball bat and chased the tall kid all around the schoolyard until the teachers stopped it and took the bat and sent us all to class it was a melting pot school where we had been dumped by the new york city board of education because the last school we attended was a bit wild with vandalism and gangs which upset a lot of the parents because we were the bright kids who were supposed to finish both seventh and eighth grades in one year but they had not finished building the school yet so we did not have full days of class until after new years which made us pretty darn bright because we finished both grades in a half year and at that rate we might graduate high school before completing puberty but someone must have complained because for ninth grade we were deployed to another school where there were no gangs no vandalism just a principal who did not want us in her stew because maybe we did not fit her recipe and maybe we were a bit indigestible so her plan seemed to be to burn us before any melting could occur and isn't it great this american pastime of bats and balls and watching the big guy take a fall unless you're a yankee fan which most of us were being from the bronx and all and the principal must have been a great yankee fan because she certainly loved beating up on us little guys that she didn't want ruining her nice school so she found a homeroom for us wherever space allowed in home ec on the floor in the gym and finally in the shop where she let us live out the remainder of our wonderful year at her delightful institution after decimating our class from thirty-two to sixteen by pulling a few very clever tricks like having us retake the reading test because our grades were too high and declaring eighty-five the passing grade and making us stay after every day for extra classes even though it was not our fault that we spent the previous year at a school which was under construction and where gangs beat up anyone who wasn't violent and she wasn't nice about it either just came into the room one day and read off a list of names of kids who were being kicked out of the academically advanced program and being sent back to eighth grade in their respective ghetto schools where they could join gangs or get beat up or make themselves invisible which sent one of the girls crying and screaming down the hallway but what did the principal care she was just a little girl from some other neighborhood and this is america this is social darwinism only the strong survive only the toughest piece of meat does not get chewed like that short kid with his baseball bat that they took away but they couldn't stop him and after school he took out a baseball from his pocket and chased the tall kid all the way to the train station and is that not america's pastime the big guys beating on the little guys the little guys beating on the big guys and the spectators laughing glad they're not getting beat up and just hoping to survive

yankee fan

my cap is navy blue and boldly embroidered
with white interlocking letters
i bought it in my old neighborhood in the bronx
five bucks at a store on creston avenue
a converted newsstand that sells
handbags trinkets statues umbrellas
everything but candy and newspapers
yes the kids and i have inherited
my mother's love for a good bargain
and her loyalty to the home team
but the yankees are always on the road when we visit
so we cruise dollar stores and discount joints
and watch the game on television
and watch grandma watching the game
rooting for hits and home runs
putting whammies on opposing pitchers
screaming with the intensity
of a green bay packers fan when the bears are losing
and i wear my new york yankees baseball cap
all over madison wisconsin
where everyone is so politically correct
and motivated by humanitarianism or legislation
taught from childhood not to hurt anyone's feelings
and these friendly and sensitive midwesterners
are compelled to say hello to passersby
even those wearing new york yankee caps
but like some landlocked progeny
of the ancient mariner they must catch my eye
and tell me with compulsive conviction
that they hate the yankees
and i must smile and listen
to these hardworking middle americans
as they denounce good old american capitalism
at least as it applies to winning teams

but i am too polite to tell them
i mostly wear the cap to keep the sun out of my eyes
though i do have some recall
of kubek boyer and richardson
and an aging mantle hitting a home run
three balls two strikes two outs
in the bottom of the ninth *holy cow*
and mel stottlemyre's inside-the-park grand slam
but i was too young to understand the game
and when i was old enough to appreciate baseball
the yanks were so bad they had rocky colavito pitch
and the best catch i saw at the stadium
was made by a fat i mean overweight
i mean corporally-gifted woman
she had a straw hat three feet in diameter
and when the foul ball bounced off a box seat rail
she held up her hat and it went right in
she might have been from the midwest
or the grand concourse and who knows
where she bought that oversized beach hat
and that magnificent muumuu
the fans applauded the beauty of it
finally something to cheer about
and the right field grandstand
gave her a standing ovation
we wanted to offer her a contract
she was built like the bambino
and we needed a new superstar
instead we got a decade of despair
but how can i explain this to those who are compelled
to tell me that they hate the yankees
while i am compelled to listen
i who was raised in the era
before lawyers and psychologists and sensitivity training

raised in an environment so insensitive
it invented the bronx cheer
i who do not hate the cubs or the brewers
though i will not watch the braves
after all those america's team commercials
because this is america and no american
should be told who to root for
and that smiley faced cleveland indians' logo
is too offensive even for my politically incorrect taste
but i do not explain this
it would take too long and these friendly
fellow americans might ask
about my brooklyn accent
even though i am from the bronx
just like the yankees so i let them talk
and when their strange power of speech
is done and they are once again
congenial madisonians
i simply reply
the more you hate us the more we love it
the more you boo us the more fun it is to win

Author's Commentary: Initial Ideas and Inspiration

The centerpiece of this poem is the great catch made in the right field box seats by a lady with an oversized straw hat. She received an ovation from the amazed spectators. In the final year of his career, Rocky Colavito, an outfielder, played for the Yankees; I really did get see him take the field as a relief pitcher. My father sometimes got free tickets to the games, and I remember, quite vividly, sitting behind home plate when an aging Mickey Mantle, with bad knees and broad shoulders, hit the game winning home run on a 3-2-2 count in the bottom of the ninth.

My mother was an avid Yankee fan. She almost saw Babe Ruth play, but she was late getting home from school, so her father took her sister to the game instead. She almost got Joe DiMaggio's autograph; she was next in line, but the police officer turned her away. During one of her years in high school, her classes ended at noon on Fridays. She, and a few friends, and one of her teachers, went to the ballpark. They alternated between the Polo Grounds, if the Giants were in town, and Yankee Stadium, if the Yankees were in. Her teacher knew Lou Gehrig, and they sometimes sat behind the Yankee dugout.

I do not aspire to have my mother's avid passion for the Yankees, but I remember as a youngster buying a sixteen ounce bottle of Coca Cola and sitting in front of our black and white television to watch an afternoon of baseball. I saw Stottlemyre's inside the park grand slam home run, a great accomplishment for a pitcher. I drifted away from sports when I was in college, but was glad at the Yankees rebirth in the 1970s.

After moving to Wisconsin, my wife and I had a great time rooting for the Brewers, especially in the early 1980s, but their World Series run was followed by decades of mediocrity, and the highlight of their games became Bob Uecker's narrative.

When I went back to The Bronx to visit Mom, she listened to or watched the Yankee games, and I became a fan again. I still am, but not to the extent that she was. When she moved in with us, we sometimes listened to the games together, and I cherish the memories, especially our excitement when the Yankees swept Boston in a five game series.

In Madison, I wore the baseball cap to shade my eyes. But as nice as the Madisonians are—and I do enjoy having lived here for over four decades—some did feel compelled to tell me that they hated the Yankees. Most of them forgave me when I told them that I grew up in The Bronx, about two-and-a-half miles from the Stadium.

Author's Notes: Revision and Retrospection

The process of revision included adding my mother to the opening section and checking my facts. Mel Stottlemyer did not hit a World Series home run. But on July 20, 1965, he hit an inside-the park grand slam into Yankee Stadium's Death Valley. I saw it on television, and probably confused that memorable moment with watching Stottlemyre pitch in the 1964 World Series.

yankee fan (6/25/04)

i wear my cap
the dark blue one embroidered with the white oversized NY
i bought for five bucks at an asian store on creston avenue
one of those converted newsstands that sells handbags and trinkets
statues and umbrellas and everything but candy and newspapers
like many shops on fordham road now do which makes
trips to the bronx interesting and i wear it
all over madison wisconsin where everyone is so
politically correct and motivated
by humanitarianism or legislation not to hurt
anyone's feelings but these friendly
and sensitive midwesterners are compelled to say hello
and like some landlocked progeny of the ancient mariner
they must catch my eye and tell me
with compulsive conviction that they hate the yankees
and i must smile and listen
to these hardworking middle americans
as they denounce good old american capitalism
at least as it applies to winning teams
but i am too polite to tell them
i mostly wear the cap to keep the sun out of my eyes
though i do have some recall
of kubek boyer and richardson
and an aging mantle hitting a home run
three balls two strikes two outs in the bottom of the ninth
to win the game and mel stottlemyre's world series home run
but i was too young to understand the game

and when i was old enough to really appreciate baseball
the yanks were so bad they had rocky colavito pitch
and the best catch i saw at the stadium
was made by a fat i mean overweight i mean corporally gifted woman
she had a straw hat with a three foot diameter and when the foul ball
bounced off a box seat rail and headed toward the field she held up her hat
the ball went right in
she might have been from the midwest but the fans
applauded the beauty of it
a standing ovation and we wanted to offer her a contract
but how can i explain this to those who are compelled to tell me
that they hate the yankees
while i am compelled to listen
i who was raised
in the era before lawyers and psychologists
in an environment so insensitive it invented the bronx cheer
i who do not hate
the cubs or the brewers or even the white sox
though i will not watch the braves
after all those america's team commercials
because this is america
and no american should be told who to root for
and that smiley faced cleveland indians' logo is too much
even for my politically incorrect taste
but i do not explain this
it would take too long and these friendly
fellow americans might ask
about my brooklyn accent even though i'm from the bronx
just like the yankees
so i let them talk and when their strange power of speech
is done and they are once again
congenial madisonians
i keep my cool and simply reply
the more you boo us the more fun it is to win
the more you hate us
the more
we enjoy it

the gambling leaguers

cheer of crowd crack of bat slap of leather
what beauty in the grace of the great
in the arc of arm of ball of leaping body
the skillful passion of these sandlot ballers
these gambling leaguers these seasonal warriors
waging serious sport in parks and playgrounds
on diamonds of clay or asphalt
against a background of bridge and school
of factory and tenement
a colorful panorama of the ordinary
no one asks for autographs
just victory over the tedium of work and bills
and the urban summer's ceaseless heat
this childhood game fought with adult intensity
for stakes of fifty or a hundred per position or more
side bets among spectators and the excitement begins
the fans live and die in suspense
the winners are rich the losers poor
celebration and frustration and the promise
of the next game the next season
so they play till the money runs out
till legs no longer run till arms no longer throw
with the speed and strength of youth and they fade
into the bleachers to wait
to play again perhaps
where summer is eternal
and the umpires
omniscient

Author's Commentary: Initial Ideas and Inspiration

When I was a young teen, my friend's uncle took us to play on Randall's Island. When we got to the fence around the parking lot, he put both of his hands on it, lifted up, turned his body ninety degrees, and landed gracefully on the other side. He was over forty years old. I was amazed. I was told he was an athlete who played ball in games where betting occurred. I never attended one of those games, but I tried in this poem to imagine what it would have been like to do so.

Author's Notes: Revision and Retrospection

An earlier version of the poem was published in 1994 in *The Glacier Stopped Here: an anthology of poems by Dane County Writers*.

the gambling leaguers (1994)

thus eternal youth fulfill the american dream
president and millionaire would trade all
for a few hot seasons on a winning team
a crisp uniform a sunny blue afternoon
the stark illumination of a muggy summer night
cheer of crowd crack of bat slap of leather
the game that could last forever if the pitching held
a battle of statistics and manipulating odds
win more than lose to stay ahead
what beauty in the grace of the great
in the arc of arm of ball of leaping body
sketched upon diamonds and the skillful passion
of these sandlot softballers our truly free agents
never to play before caesar in yankee stadium
only the umpire's thumb reveals their fate
these gambling leaguers these seasonal warriors
waging serious sport in parks and playgrounds
the childhood game fought with adult ferocity
against a background of bridge and school
of factory and tenement a colorful postcard
of the ordinary and no one asks autographs
just victory over despair
on land investors don't want or can't buy at fifty
or a hundred per position or more

sidebets among spectators all serious to win
stake the rent on a big game and root for the best
the winners are rich the losers poor
any game may redistribute the wealth
the fans live and die in suspense
rookies and veterans perpetually prepare
it takes years of hustling to make a good team
and like the politician like the entrepreneur
they play till the money runs out
till legs no longer run till arms no longer throw
and vanish in the memory of glory

lost again on old subways

i am lost again on old subways
at third avenue station the lights go out
the lunatic laughs
the lunatic who does not appear
until the lights go out
and i cannot see him
and i cannot see what he is laughing at
he laughs and he laughs
death is solemn
but suffering is hysterical
when it happens to others
the three fates the three stooges
torturing each other while the children laugh
until the lights go out and they are stuck
in their own nightmares
and he laughs at my fear
and i laugh at him laughing at my fear
because i am afraid not to
keep the lunatic happy
i have paid my fare and i must journey
there is nowhere to go but where the darkness takes me
and i must get my money's worth
the doors will not open
i cannot depart at the home station
and i slip past my sleeping parents
under the bronx and over the bronx
all the unseen passengers on this runaway train
are laughing and laughing
because we are afraid to stop
we are lost in the bronx
where guns will not save us
and the churches are closed for the night
and the candles lit for the souls of the dead
have burned out and the priests

have locked the rectories
and we are laughing too hard to pray
and we are laughing so hard we almost enjoy it
we have transformed we are the laughing commuters
of the IRT which never looked so good
though we cannot see it as it trembles on
through the night which does not stop
through strange territories where strangers lurk
in the shadows waiting for a few laughs

Author's Commentary: Initial Ideas and Inspiration

I seem to remember being on the Pelham Bay train when its lights went out at the Third Avenue station. That event may have appeared later in a dream, but I do think it really happened. I also had a dream in which I was on the train but could not get off. I do not remember if the laughter occurred in reality or in my dream.

Author's Notes: Revision and Retrospection

From my notebook (February, 1990) written after the dream:

riding on an empty subway train
we pull into third avenue 138th street
and the lights go out
this is a dream i had last night
riding on a blind subway train
it was spooky because i was going to the wrong
part of the bronx and would never get home
without going all the way back
and getting on the right train
and i wasn't alone at all
i was standing or sitting before or beside
a strange knapsack with many pockets
which folded out to have

a sink in the middle
and i wasn't alone
there was a laughing lunatic
somewhere in the darkness of the closed door subway car
as it wound through the black tunnel and rose
in the dark night

These lines appear on the next page; they suggest that I did not get on the 4 train at 125th Street, but stayed on the Pelham Bay train.

riding the subway home
i do not get off at 125th street
i do not get on the right train
that will take me to my new home
and i don't know why i don't
so i wind up back in the south bronx
the train pulls into the third avenue station
which was always deserted
and the lights go out
this is all a dream i had last night
riding in a blind subway train
i was all alone but was not

In November, 1990 I came up with these lines:

the subway stops between stations
an empty car the lights flicker out
night slips in through the tunnel
the laughing lunatic laughs
and laughs as though the night
were terribly silly
you have no newspaper to hide behind
and the doors are locked

As I worked on the poem, I focused on the darkness and the laughter. And on an image that I had of the train flying over my parents' apartment and St. Luke's Church. A surreal image, as the 6 train ran underground through my old neighborhood. The image may have been part of the dream. Or just my imagination.

randall's island

I

here the sky is blue and the water dark
and the bronx an invisible memory
here clouds roll off the continent
goodbye goodbye go rain upon the old world
should it still exist

here the new city greets ancient tides
at the corner of harlem and hell gate
and distinctions obscure
where is the end where is the beginning
how many have drowned like names in the wind

chaotic currents chaotic streets
the orderly megalithic shoreline
of a fishdead metropolis
a horizontal stonehenge on which to celebrate
existence and the rats seem to dance

i cast my bait into the emptiness
launch my kite to the sun
no fish to catch no one to meet
this is a forgotten island
obscure as childhood

II

the confluence of memory and dream
this prehistoric erosion from the mainland
a muddle of time and amazing eternity
there are moments when dandelions roar
in sunlight like british muskets

when summer grass shimmers
as if the present were luminous
while churning and dark the currents
muffle all sound and the unheard
skyline rises to the unspeaking heavens

the delinquent cursed at toil and at play
the institutionalized soul
screamed with rage and frustration
in the infants' hospital the foundling cried
and succumbed to quiet death

the house of refuge the idiot asylum the orphanage
razed and forgotten
and the triborough bridge rises
above park and playground and stadium
amid the wayward whispers of these outcast lands

III

green ticket booths and silver railings
the bleachers are empty and in the plaza
the bronze discus thrower stands naked and alone
trimmed hedges low walls red brick
i balance between fantasy and failure

beneath the pillars of the viaduct
i learn my clumsy insignificance
this is a sacred place and we bury
songless parakeets in shoe boxes after they die
and launch plastic rockets to the virgin moon

between fact and delusion the line has vanished
the little hell gate has drowned in the garbage landfill
the bridge to the psychiatric hospital
stands irrelevant over a river of grass
and rabbits run mad across evening fields

what insane dreams wander the wasteland
darkness drizzles and night
awakens the restless tenements
wisps of arson smog the horizon and i must return
i must and it seems

even i am not here

Author's Commentary: Initial Ideas and Inspiration

According to my ruler and my map, Randall's Island is 1.5 inches from the apartment where I grew up, about a half mile as the pigeon flies. The direct route would require walking south to the end of Brook Avenue at 132nd Street, crossing the rail yards, and crossing a creek called the Bronx Kill. Sometimes, on a weekday, my mother walked me to Cypress Avenue and over the Bronx span of the Triborough Bridge which had stairs that accessed the island. She took me to the playground which was supervised by a gray-haired Black matron attired in what appeared to be a nurse's white dress. Her name was Willie, and Mom said she liked me because my name was William. Mom and Willie enjoyed their chats, and I enjoyed the park's amenities. Willie might turn on the water in the wading pool even though there were no other children in the playground. She might take out basketballs or horseshoes for me to play with. There never seemed to be many other people around.

Sometimes my aunt and cousins came along. On the weekends, or maybe on a summer evening, Dad drove us there. He parked in the shade beneath the viaduct of the Triborough Bridge. It was a good spot to wash and wax the car. Sometimes I helped, and sometimes I played around the pillars. They were massive, tall, formidable supports for the deck on which cars buses and trucks passed unceasingly and unseen overhead. Standing beneath them makes one feel small, insignificant, perhaps.

East of the Triborough was a large oval parking lot. It usually was empty, as we did not usually go to Randall's Island when there was a sporting event or a concert at the stadium. Occasionally a marching band practiced there: a good choice, as the parking area seemed to be as large as a football field. Beyond that was the Hell Gate Railroad Bridge. Another massive structure. Another engineering masterpiece. Sometimes we counted the cars of the very long freight trains as they slowly but steadily passed.

Randall's Island enthralled me. There were broad open lawns. There were trees. There was a willow on the northwest side that I climbed once or twice. The island was lined with large flat stones. We stood on them and watched the Harlem River flow into the East River while Manhattan loomed quietly in the background.

Randall's Island was separated from Ward's Island by the Little Hell Gate. Randall's Island was a park. Ward's Island housed the Manhattan Psychiatric Institute and a center for the criminally insane. When I was young, Ward's Island was separated from Randall's Island and could be accessed by a bridge which had a security guard post. What mysteries lay beyond the seldom-travelled bridge?

Now, the islands have been connected by landfill.

The juxtaposition of the Harlem River meeting with the turbulent currents of the Hell Gate, and of the imagined horrors of Ward's Island, with the bucolic trees and fields and innocent playground of Randall's Island, made this a place as fascinating to me as the Xanadu described in Coleridge's "Kubla Khan."

I have not been there in fifty years. It remains in my memory as a place of peace and wonder.

Author's Notes: Revision and Retrospection

From the 1996 version to the final, there were a few changes to the first section. The second section underwent much revision; I took out references to the colonial history and included the island's subsequent use as home to a house of refuge for juvenile delinquents, a foundling hospital, and an idiot asylum—as it was called at the time. Until Robert Moses came along, the island was a place for the unwanted. In the 1930s, Moses had the institutions closed and converted the island into a park with a stadium for athletic events. Downing Stadium opened in time to host the Olympic trials in 1936, and was venue to a variety of sports and music events over the years.

The early and final versions of the third section of the poem begin in the same place: the plaza outside the stadium. Both versions include similar imagery: the parakeet, the filling-in of the Little Hell Gate, the psychiatric hospital, the irrelevant bridge. And the rabbits. I was fascinated when I saw a rabbit run across a field on the island one evening as we drove home. Most parks in New York City had squirrels. But a real live wild rabbit! Wow!

The research that led to the early version of Randall's Island's was done from *The Bronx and Its People: A History 1609—1927*. I came across it at the Wisconsin Historical Society Library, and after it was removed from their collection, I purchased the three volume set, which I found on the internet. The internet also gave me information about the post-colonial history of Randall's Island. And about how this paradise of my youth has been transformed into a sports complex, with a golf driving range, tennis center, and over sixty athletic fields.

I prefer to remember it as it was when I was young.

randall's island (9-11-96)

I

here the sky is blue and the water dark
and the bronx invisible
here clouds roll off the continent
goodbye goodbye and rain upon the old world
if it still exists

here the city meets ancient tides
at the corner of harlem and hell gate
distinctions obscure
where is the end where the beginning
how many have drowned like names in the wind

chaotic currents chaotic streets
an orderly megalithic shoreline

curbs the wrestling rivers
of the fishdead metropolis
rats dance on this fallen stonehenge

i cast my line into the emptiness
launch my kite to the sun
there is no one to meet
this is a forgotten island
inconvenient as childhood

even i am not here

II

the confluence of memory and dream
a prehistoric erosion from the mainland
time is a muddle
of dandelions roaring in
sunlight
the west wind the shimmering patient grass

ghost canoes wander the wampum shores
an economy of periwinkle broken
by dutch counterfeiters the guns
of revolution line the muddy kill
wayward boys drift from destitute studies

the great bridge born of the great depression
immigrant artisans craft this park
fight in wars move to the suburbs
the flag flies in the asphalt plaza
gray and empty

this is american soil conquered and paid for
with blood with wealth with concrete and steel
the rise and the fall of the beautiful bronx
what wetlands what woodlands what whispers
of lost life hush these broad lawns

wisps of arson smog the horizon

III

trimmed hedges low walls red brick
i balance between fantasy and failure
no one sees my awkwardness
green ticket booths silver railings
herd the crowd which is not here

to games which are not happening
the bronze discus thrower is naked and alone
new deal art lost in the new age
the sleeping stadium awaits its heroes
there is solitude in the multitude of the city

there is solitude on this vacuum of an island
beneath the pillars of the triborough bridge
i learn insignificance
in this sacred place we bury
parakeets in shoe boxes when they die

while feasting gulls circle and caw
the seasons pass the garbage landfill
closes the little hell gate its furious waters
beat the irrelevant bridge to the psychiatric hospital
what insane dreams wander the wasteland

darkness drizzles and rabbits run mad across evening fields
night awakens the tenements and i am not here
wisps of arson smog the horizon and i must return
i must

triborough bridge: suspension

    the

    sky

    road rises

    quickly above green

    shores and gray waters

from astoria to wards island from anchorage to massive anchorage

    graceful cables curve

    sturdy

    blue

    arches

    crowned

    with art deco lanterns

atop steel towers that aspire to heaven above the turbulent hell gate

    bearing the stress of humanity

    festooning the night

    with man

    made

    stars

Author's Commentary: Initial Ideas and Inspiration

The original poem, "triborough bridge," was published in 1996. When I worked on *from the banks of brook avenue,* I decided not only to revise it, but to expand it. The expansion seemed to be best executed as a series of four poems. This is the first. Because it is a concrete poem that attempts to recapture the shape of the bridge, it seemed appropriate to use the word "suspension" in the title.

Author's Notes: Revision and Retrospection

Much of the writing process involved getting the words and phrases into a form that could re-create the shape of the bridge. The description had to be accurate, and I used the internet to look at photos of the bridge, over and over again, and to read about the terms used to describe its structure.

I chose to present the poem vertically because I needed a one-page poem to make the transition from "randall's island" to "stasis." Limiting "suspension" to a singe page would allow "stasis" to begin on the left page and continue on the right.

If the reader turns the page sideways, the shape of the bridge appears. The early version of the poem below was too long to fit vertically on a single page. Closing the space between the lines would not do, as the shape of the bridge would not be as obvious, at least not to my eye, so the final version required me to cut two lines: "sun and storm" and "atop two ornamental towers." The word "cathedral" also was removed.

Note: the 2015 version that appears in on the following page is in a smaller font size than the one used in *from the banks of brook avenue.*

triborough bridge suspension span (6/8/15)

the

sky

road rises

quickly above green

shores and gray waters

from astoria to wards island from anchorage to massive anchorage

through sun and storm

graceful cables curve

sturdy

blue

arches

crowned

with art deco lanterns

atop two ornamental towers

steel cathedrals that aspire to heaven above the turbulent hell gate

bearing the stress of humanity

festooning the night

with man

made

stars

triborough bridge: stasis

where is everybody going
the best part of this bridge is the middle
between here and there
between above and below
between all the points
on the invisible compass
of our existence
between scylla and charybdis
to the east the solemn frown
of the railroad bridge over the bucolic hell gate
to the west the land of opportunity and misfortune
the magnificent skyline
a forest of penthouse and project
where the homeless home in the shadows
humanity is beautiful from a distance
the landfills bloom with green growth
frivolous waves drown the effluence
of the money mad world
to the north the sewage treatment plant
that will never make us clean
and the manhattan psychiatric hospital
and the center for the criminally insane
and the abandoned asylum
where inmates laughed at pedestrians
as they walked across the sky
in the longago days of carefree strolls
before random violence
before muggings in broad daylight
the happy people of wards island
picnic beneath trees
to the south children splash
in the clear blue water of astoria pool
imagining that they are sharks
or whales or submarines

imagining that summer will never end
reality is such an imposition
like the grim stone of the war memorial
just beyond their youthful laughter
and above restless clouds drive by
on their ceaseless commute
below there is bedlam and mayhem and the tides
swirl over suicides and shipwrecks
but here in the middle there is peace
there is stasis
there is the music
of wind murmuring through cables
why must every polluted river be crossed
here words are invisible
and the past is no more
the future is but the loss of the present
leap to the sky
not to fly
jump to the water
never to swim again
walk ashore
to live and die in the eternal city
where the meek await to inherit
what is left of the earth
o the hovering the hovering

Author's Commentary: Initial Ideas and Inspiration

This poem is an elaboration of the original "triborough bridge." Perhaps "stasis" originated in a childhood event. When I visiting Nana's house, my cousin, who lived with her, was going to the park to exercise, and he took me along. When my mother found out that he was not going to the nearby Saint Mary's Park, but was going to walk to the end of Cypress Avenue and then across the Triborough Bridge to Astoria Park in Queens, she ran after us for several blocks to retrieve me.

Perhaps it was best that Mom intervened, as I somehow acquired a fear of heights. Perhaps I would not have acquired a fear of heights had she not intervened. Or maybe I just would have panicked. But things are what they are.

So I did not go to Astoria Park with my cousin, and I never walked across the bridge. But in writing this poem, I imagine what it would be like to stand on that walkway, in the very middle of the suspension span, with Manhattan in the distance.

In her youth, my mother enjoyed walking on the Triborough and looking at the Manhattan skyline from the pedestrian path. Once, while walking on the bridge, she heard the screams of the patients in the psychiatric facilities. That image became part of the poem.

We drove over the Triborough innumerable times, going to Astoria Pool or to LaGuardia Airport, so the imagery is vivid in my mind: the Hell Gate Bridge to the east, Manhattan to the west, Ward's Island to the north, and Astoria Pool to the south. Given all of that detail, the subtitle, "stasis," seemed appropriate.

Author's Notes: Revision and Retrospection

The original version appeared in *POETS <u>on the line</u>* in 1996:

triborough bridge (1996)

where is everybody going
the best part of this bridge is the middle
between blue heaven and swirling hellgate
here the wind murmurs through cables
and words are invisible
why must every polluted river be crossed

i savor the land for what it is
the primordial musk of the imagination
gone money mad
skyline of penthouse and project
life submerged behind tiny windows
like stars in the sleepless city night
o the homeless home beneath broad buttresses
beyond obscure shorelines
yes even humanity seems beautiful from a distance
green growth upon landfills
i can't see the sewage for the waves
the sanitation plant the abandoned asylum
where lunatics laughed at pedestrians
long gone the days of open windows
where i never walked
reality is an imposition
the manhattan psychiatric hospital
stares at my feet
wards island park
misfits picnic beneath trees
if sanity permits
o the suicidal tides
the war memorial
on the astorian shore
the past is no more
the future is but the loss of the present
leap to the sky
i'll not fly
jump to the water
never to swim again
walk ashore
i live and die in the eternal city
where the meek await to inherit
what is left of the earth
o the hovering the hovering

The following revision in June, 2015 adds "between the above and the below" and "to the east . . . to the west." This is a stepping-stone to the poem's final direction.

triborough bridge: the catwalk (6/12/15)

where is everybody going
the best part of this bridge is the middle
between the war memorial
and the manhattan psychiatric hospital
between the above and the below
to the east the grim smile
of the railroad bridge over the bucolic hellgate
to the west the land of opportunity
and misfortune
here the wind murmurs through cables
and words are invisible
why must every polluted river be crossed
savor the land for what it is
the primordial musk of the imagination
gone money mad
the magnificent skyline
a forest of penthouse and project
where homeless home in the shadows
humanity is beautiful from a distance
the landfills bloom with green growth
frivolous waves drown the sewage
the sanitation plant the abandoned asylum
where lunatics laughed at pedestrians
as they walked across the sky
in the longago days
of carefree strolls
in wards island park
happy people picnic beneath trees
if sanity permits
reality is an imposition
the past is no more
the future is but the loss of the present
leap to the sky
not to fly
jump to the water
never to swim again
walk ashore
to live and die in the eternal city

where the meek await to inherit
what is left of the earth
o the hovering the hovering

By September, 2015, "stasis" is included in the title; the term seems to capture the focus of the poem.

triborough bridge: stasis (9/13/15)

where is everybody going
the best part of this bridge is the middle
between here and there
between above and below
between all the points
on the invisible compass
of our existence
between scylla and charibdis
to the east the grim smile
of the railroad bridge over the bucolic hellgate
to the west the land of opportunity and misfortune
the magnificent skyline
a forest of penthouse and project
where the homeless home in the shadows
humanity is beautiful from a distance
the landfills bloom with green growth
and frivolous waves drown the effluence
of the money mad world
to the north the sewage treatment plant
that will never make us clean
and the manhattan psychiatric hospital
and the center for the criminally insane
and the abandoned asylum
where inmates laughed at pedestrians
as they walked across the sky
in the longago days of carefree strolls
before random violence

and muggings in broad daylight
and the happy people of wards island
picnic beneath trees
to the south children splash
in the clear blue water of astoria pool
imagining that they are sharks
or whales or submarines
imagining that summer will never end
reality is such an imposition
like the grim stone of the war memorial
just beyond their youthful laughter
above the clouds drive by
on their ceaseless commute
below there is bedlam and mayhem and the tides
swirl over suicides and shipwrecks
but here in the middle is peace and stasis and the music
of wind murmuring through cables
why must every polluted river be crossed
here words are invisible
and the past is no more
the future is but the loss of the present
leap to the sky
not to fly
jump to the water
never to swim again
walk ashore
to live and die in the eternal city
where the meek await to inherit
what is left of the earth
o the hovering the hovering

triborough bridge: genesis

in the beginning there was the land and the water
the water separated the mainland from the islands
and moses said *may there be a great bridge*
to join the islands to the islands and the islands to the mainland
it was good and moses said
may there be roads and highways that lead to the great bridge
that joins the islands to the islands and the islands to the mainland
it was good and moses said
may there be parks and playgrounds
for the people in the cars that drive
on the roads and highways that lead to the great bridge
that joins the islands to the islands and the islands to mainland
it was good and moses said
may there be money to build the great bridge
and the roads and highways and parks and playgrounds
and behold there was money
the nation went to work and it was good
the steel industry lit its furnaces and factories reopened
loggers logged and sawmills sawed
railroads hauled lumber across the continent
laborers constructed wooden forms and poured cement
barges ferried girders over the water and towers rose
cables were wound and anchored
the deck suspended and the roadway paved
the great bridge joined the islands to the islands
and the islands to the mainland
there were parks and parkways and the president
came for the opening ceremony
and the people came and rushed to be first
to pay the toll and cross the great bridge
and more people came to pay the toll
more people and more money
money that could be used to build more bridges
and it was all good
but moses did not rest

Author's Commentary: Initial Ideas and Inspiration

The construction of the Triborough Bridge during the Great Depression was a project of massive proportions, and I tried to recapture some of its grand scope. Robert Moses was the impetus behind the bridge, and all that went with it: access roads, parkways, Astoria Pool, and Randall's Island's conversion into a park. In 1932, the initial effort to build the bridge came to a halt. Moses took over, and the bridge opened in 1936.

Moses is associated with innumerable projects in the New York metropolitan area. One of them, which is not mentioned in this poem, is the Cross Bronx Expressway, a project which split The Bronx in two, an event which some critics attribute to the decline of the borough. In another poem, "welcome to the mainland," I mention this: "and moses parts the land / his great road cleaves its heart / there is exodus poverty turmoil and tragedy . . ."

The analogy to the parting of the Red Sea led to my echoing Genesis. Hence, the poem's title. And the tone. And its last lines.

Author's Notes: Revision and Retrospection

This is an earlier version. The final version eliminated many unnecessary uses of the word "and." Italics were added to help the reader through the poem. In this case, the italics do not indicate anything directly stated by any being, mortal or otherwise. But based on my research, they seem appropriate to this fictionalized speaker.

triborough bridge: genesis (June, 2015)

in the beginning there was the land and the water
and the water separated the mainland from the islands
and moses said may there be a great bridge

to join the islands to the islands and the islands to mainland
and it was good and moses said
may there be roads and highways to lead to the great bridge
that joins the islands to the islands and the islands to mainland
and it was good and moses said
may there be parks and playgrounds
for the people in the cars that drive
on the roads and highways that lead to the great bridge
that joins the islands to the islands and the islands to mainland
and it was good and moses said
may there be money to build the great bridge
and the roads and highways and parks and playgrounds
and behold there was money
and the nation went to work and it was good
and steel mills lit their furnaces
and cement factories reopened
and forests were felled to make forms for the cement
and barges were lashed together to carry girders over the water
and towers rose and cables were wound and anchored
and the great bridge joined the islands to the islands
and the islands to mainland and there were parks and parkways
and the president came for the opening ceremony
and the people came and rushed to be first
to pay the toll and cross the bridge
and more people kept coming
to pay the toll and cross the bridge
and more people came and more money
money that could be used to build more bridges
and moses looked down
and it was all good
but he did not rest

triborough bridge: kinesis

an automobile vortex
where three bridges meet
twelve directions of traffic
twenty-two lanes that do not intersect
cars can go from here to there to another there
this is america and there are tolls
to pay and toll booths to collect the money
and police to collect those who do not pay the toll
but we kids are oblivious to the wonders of engineering
and we have no money to give to trolls
we run and scream and fight monsters
in the cement towers of the bronx span
we want to ascend the spooky staircase
and explore the walkway to manhattan
but mommy herds us to the playground on randall's island
where she can sit in the shade and talk to the matron
while the cars whirl overhead
and harry sits on his hill
a small patch of grass bordered by an access ramp
beneath the grand junction
where the harlem span meets the viaduct
harry in his undershirt
drinking his quart of beer hidden in a brown paper bag
basking in the sun and alone in the quiet
he does not build bridges
he does not have a car
he works hard and dies in poverty
they give his ashes to the winds
and he intersects
with everywhere in the great universe
as cars speed by
and the commuters take no notice

Author's Commentary: Initial Ideas and Inspiration

Harry, not his real name, was not burly in stature, but he had a physically demanding job which included loading trucks. He had a reputation for being a hard worker. When time or weather permitted, he sunned himself on a small hill on Randall's Island; the small hill, delineated by an access road, was beneath the intersection of the Manhattan lift bridge, the Bronx truss bridge, and the viaduct to the Queens suspension bridge. It was adjacent to the Randall's Island police station, so it was a safe place to relax. Randall's Island also housed the Administration Building from which Robert Moses ran the Triborough Bridge and Tunnel Authority. Like Moses, Harry did not drive a car. Unlike Moses, Harry did not build bridges. He was just an ordinary guy.

Author's Notes: Revision and Retrospection

This version is from June, 2015. Early notes were tentatively titled "octopus" and "flying junction." I finally decided upon "kinesis," as the word suggested movement and fit with the other titles in the sequence.

As the poem evolved, I tweaked some of the wording, and changed the last eight lines from past to present tense. The addition of the line: "and we have no money to give to trolls" seemed appropriate to the context of childhood play.

triborough bridge: kinesis (June, 2015)

an automobile vortex
where three bridges meet
its design is an act of genius
twelve directions of traffic
twenty two lanes that do not intersect
cars can go from here to there to another there
but this is america and there are tolls

to pay and toll booths to collect the money
and police to collect those
who do not pay the toll
but we are kids and oblivious
to the wonders of engineering
when we walk the bronx span to randall's island
we run and scream and play
in the cement towers
and we want to ascend the spooky staircase
and explore the walkway to manhattan
but mommy herds us to playground
where she can sit in the shade and talk to the matron
while the cars whirl overhead
and harry sits on his hill
a small patch of grass bordered by an access ramp
beneath the grand junction
where the harlem span t-bones the viaduct
harry in this undershirt
drinking his quart of beer hidden
in a brown paper bag
basking in the sun
alone in the quiet
he did not build bridges
he did not have a car
he worked hard and died in poverty
they gave his ashes to the winds
and he intersected
with everywhere
in the great universe
and the cars sped by
and did not notice

astoria park

the memorial is a tombstone
gray as war
gray as the hell gate's insane tides
gray as the triborough's symmetry
gray as the psychiatric hospital's lobotomized windows
gray as the railroad's commerce
gray as the skyline of the glorious city
gray as the storm we watched
father and son from the concrete bleachers
the crowd ran from the pool
raindrops splashed on the chlorine
we sat in the gray rain
we sat together

the dead are not buried here
they are gone as are the dolphins
which led the dutchman up this strait
intoxication and shipwreck
visions of the devil dancing on his stones
new amsterdam is gone
the indians are gone
this east river is toxic
it flows north and south
it never was a river
daddy tells stories of sunken treasure ships
we will never be rich
we will never be but what we are

father and son
forever in the gray rain
with our pot bellies and our pale skin
and our tender feet and our anxieties
our lifetimes of work and responsibility
maybe the car window is open

maybe the apartment is burning down
maybe the boss does not like us
and we will be sucked into homeless poverty
like locker keys into hungry drains beneath waveless waters
our possessions lost in bureaucracy
in america where the rivers are poison
and there are no free swims

this pool was built for the huddled masses
doff those work clothes and be free
bathing suit naked
beneath the lightning before the wind
in a distant memory of childhood
the iron bars keep us safe
we will not walk into the wine dark tides
of the hell gate and never return
we simply do not leave
at night underwater lights shine
like the new jerusalem
the gray sky darkens with stars
the spirit rises over radiant water

we simply will not leave

Author's Commentary: Initial Ideas and Inspiration

My father worked long hours at a high stress job. One of my most precious memories is of the day he took me to Astoria Pool. Just Dad and me. Mom stayed home. Having some time alone with Dad made this a very special day for me. And it rained. We sat on the cement bleachers and watched the rain. We did not stay past dark, and, of course, we eventually did leave, but the exaggeration seemed to work in the poem, and there is a part of me that is still there, with Dad.

The pool had several kiosks which emitted light beams in various directions, so at night the pool had a surreal appearance. Astoria Pool is on the north shore of Queens, just across the Hell Gate from Wards' Island. Above the pool is a concession area which offers a good view of the Hell Gate Bridge, of North Shore Drive, and of the monument which honors war veterans. The concession area has a fence with iron bars. Once one of my cousins stuck his head through them, and the fire department had to come and pry him out; perhaps the bars are still warped!

According to *Knickerbocker's History of New York,* an inebriated Dutch sailor followed dolphins up the East River and encountered the devil dancing on rocky islands in the Hell Gate. There were tales of a distant relative who did not like life in America, who wanted to return to Italy, and who committed suicide by walking off into the water. There is also the possibility that a ship, the Hussar, loaded with treasure, sank in the Hell Gate and still lies there. One of my teaching colleagues told me of a baby getting sucked into the drain of a swimming pool. All in all, from diverse sources, these images contributed to the creation of this poem.

Author's Notes: Revision and Retrospection

Some brief early notes from 1996:

at the concession stand we feast on sugar
the iron bars fence in our childhood
below us the drive curves round
the war memorial . . .
the memorial is a tombstone
gray as war
. gray as the insane waters
of the hellgate
gray as the balanced spans
of the triborough bridge
gray as the windows
of the psychiatric hospital . . .

the banks of brook avenue

and brook avenue runs
straight through the crooked world
from railroad yard
north to the meat market
and curves and disappears
into the heart of the bronx
where tenements burn and die
and stare black eyed and hollow
like the dead waiting for the soul to rise
and america flies to the moon
and america drops bombs
and america makes war on crime and drugs
but brook avenue never ends
the old mill stream flows long buried
in the great sewer beneath the great street
of the great borough of the bronx
where founding fathers sleep
beneath the shadows of saint ann's church
and indian villages deconstruct
beneath abandoned factories
and the belgian paving stones on which horses clopped
lie beneath the asphalt where automobiles drift
from the bronx kill to the american mainland
and the millbrook housing projects rise to the heavens
above tarpaper roofs where pigeons and junkies
forget their way home
and the brook babbles beneath the surface
and the brook finds its way through the underworld
to the ocean that brings
immigrants to the new continent
they build skyscrapers and railroads
they fight wars and they play baseball
they make money and move to the grand concourse
they make more money and move to the suburbs

or they remain impoverished and searching
for brook avenue grass for brook avenue women
for a steady man for a steady job
for the ship that sails to paradise
the winters are cold in unheated apartments
fire hydrants flood the summer streets with toddlers
and on the banks of brook avenue i see
the world as it is
and the sun beats down
and the bootblacks toil and sweat drops from their brows
and the bootblacks beat beauty into old shoes
and the bootblacks earn a living one dollar at a time
in america where we vote for our kings
and the police beat whom they wish
and the strong beat the weak
and the women walk to store to church to playground
and the children play beneath shady tenements
where boughs of streetlights
do not dance in the wind
and the children laugh and the children cry
on the banks of brook avenue
and the sun sets and the night rises
and the pool hall grows smoky and serious
and the children dream and the children have nightmares
and the darkness of heaven and the darkness of civilization
and the sighs of the lonely and the sighs of lovers
are indistinguishable
on the banks of brook avenue
where childhood is idyllic
and the world could not be more beautiful

Author's Commentary: Initial Ideas and Inspiration

This is the last poem of *The Bronx Trilogy*, so the collection ends where it began. Our family's shoe shine parlor was on Brook Avenue, just south of 138th Street, and it was the shoe shine parlor that inspired what I thought was my first good poem, "making it." I began to write other poems about my family, our customers, and neighborhood events. And about the sad reality of riots, overdoses, police brutality, arson, and cold apartments. As I completed my first book, *the shoe shine parlor poems et al*, I became interested in the history of The Bronx.

I was fascinated to learn that Brook Avenue lies atop a stream, the Millbrook, which was incorporated into a sewer. That image inspired the title of the poem: "the banks of brook avenue." Gouverneur Morris, who helped write the Constitution, and Lewis Morris, who signed the Declaration of Independence, are buried on the grounds of St. Ann's Episcopal Church. Morris Manor included most of the South Bronx. I sometimes tried to imagine how beautiful The Bronx must have been when it was owned by the Morris family, or in its pristine state when Jonas Bronck first came to settle there. And how beautiful it was to my grandparents and to the other immigrants who arrived there a century ago.

And I wondered how America could achieve so much while allowing its cities to fall to ruin. In the 1940s, America saved the world from tyranny and rebuilt Europe. In the 1970s, parts of the South Bronx looked like post-war Berlin. But there is hope: the brook still flows to the Bronx Kill and its unseen waters give their pittance to the Atlantic Ocean. Rebuilding has occurred: the rubble has disappeared; there are new parks and new trees and new children play in the old neighborhood. And that is beautiful.

But the shoe shine parlor is no more, and I think that bootblacks are nearing extinction. And many of the old problems still remain. Their threat slithers like a serpent through this rebuilt paradise.

Author's Notes: Revision and Retrospection

The early notes are sketchy, but of some of the images will make it into the final version.

Selected notes: the banks of brook avenue (6/14/98)

on the banks of brook avenue the old mill stream
lies buried in a great sewer beneath belgian paving stones
beneath the asphalt river where boughs of streetlights
do not dance in the wind . . .

beneath the shady tenements
brook avenue girl
brook avenue grass
the pool hall
elephants in the alley behind the puerto rico theater

and brook avenue runs
straight through the crooked world
from railroad yard
north to the meat market
and curves and disappears
into the heart of the bronx
where tenements burn and die
and stare black eyed and hollow
like the dead waiting for the soul
from the primordial slime
while america grows
we reach the moon
we fight communism
brook avenue never ends

and i was a child beneath shady tenements

an idyllic childhood beneath the shady tenements
of brook avenue . . .

on the banks of brook avenue the old mill stream
was buried in a sewer that was buried in a street
covered in paving stones and covered in asphalt

and the millbrook housing projects rise to the heavens
above the tarpaper roofs where pigeons and junkies
forget their way home . . .

on the banks of brook avenue i saw
the world as it is
and the sun beats down
our sweat fell to the ground

the horizon of tenements

and i dreamed of the old mill stream
babbling beneath the belgian paving stones
where horses clopped
long drowned in the sewer
of civilization
beneath the asphalt river where boughs of streetlights
do not dance in the wind

In this version, the first thirteen lines have emerged in final form:

the banks of brook avenue (6/23/98)

and brook avenue runs
straight through the crooked world
from railroad yard
north to the meat market
and curves and disappears
into the heart of the bronx
where tenements burn and die
and stare black eyed and hollow
like the dead waiting for the soul to rise
and america flies to the moon
and america drops bombs
and america makes war on crime and drugs
but brook avenue never ends

it twists through the capillaries of the survivors
the straight reminder that civilization
is not heaven that the world
could be more beautiful

and the old mill stream was buried
in a sewer that was buried in a street
and the belgian paving stones where horses clopped
was buried in plain asphalt
and the millbrook housing projects rise to the heavens
above the tarpaper roofs where pigeons and junkies
forget their way home
and the brook babbles beneath the surface
and the brook finds its way through the underworld
to the ocean that brings
immigrants to the new world

and on the banks of brook avenue i see
the world as it is
and the sun beat down
and we beat beauty into old shoes
we earned our living
one dollar at a time
we vote for our kings
and the police beat whom they wish
and the strong beat the weak
and the women walk to store to church to playground
and the children play beneath shady tenements
where boughs of streetlights
do not dance in the wind . . .

The next version has a direction for the poem's ending, though there will be some rearrangement of the lines in the final draft:

the banks of brook avenue (6/28/98)

. . . but brook avenue never ends
and the old mill stream lies long buried
in a great sewer beneath the great street
and the belgian paving stones where horses clopped
lie covered in asphalt where automobiles sail
from the bronx kill to the american mainland
and the millbrook housing projects rise to the heavens
above tarpaper roofs where pigeons and junkies
forget their way home

and the brook babbles beneath the surface
and the brook finds its way through the underworld
to the ocean that brings
immigrants to the new continent
and on the banks of brook avenue i see
the world as it is
and the sun beats down
and the bootblacks beat beauty into old shoes
we earn our living one dollar at a time
we vote for our kings
and the police beat whom they wish
and the strong beat the weak
and the women walk to store to church to playground
and the children play beneath shady tenements
where boughs of streetlights
do not dance in the wind
and the children laugh and the children cry
on the banks of brook avenue
where childhood is idyllic
and the world could not be more beautiful

and the sun sets and the night rises
and the darkness of heaven and the darkness of civilization
and the sighs of the lonely and the sighs of lovers

the children dream and the children wait to be born

This version elaborates on what the immigrants do and expands the lines about the bootblacks:

the banks of brook avenue (7/17/98)

. . . but brook avenue never ends
and the old mill stream lies long buried
in the great sewer beneath the great street
of the great borough of the bronx
and the founding fathers are buried beneath their gravestones
and the indian villages deconstruct beneath factories
and the belgian paving stones where horses clopped
lie covered in asphalt where automobiles drift
from the bronx kill to the american mainland

and the millbrook housing projects rise to the heavens
above tarpaper roofs where pigeons and junkies
forget their way home
and the brook babbles beneath the surface
and the brook finds its way through the underworld
to the ocean that brings
immigrants to the new continent
they build skyscrapers and railroads
they fight wars and they play baseball
they make money and move to the grand concourse
they make more money and move to the suburbs
or they remain impoverished and searching
for brook avenue grass for brook avenue women
for a steady man for a steady job
for the ship that sails to paradise
but the winters are cold in unheated apartments
and fire hydrants flood the summer streets with naked toddlers
and on the banks of brook avenue i see
the world as it is
and the sun beats down
and the bootblacks toil and sweat drops from their brows
and the bootblacks beat beauty into old shoes
and the bootblacks earn a living one dollar at a time
in america where we vote for our kings
and the police beat whom they wish
and the strong beat the weak
and the women walk to store to church to playground
and the children play beneath shady tenements
where boughs of streetlights
do not dance in the wind
and the children laugh and the children cry
on the banks of brook avenue
and the sun sets and the night rises
and the pool hall grows smoky and serious
and the children dream and the children have nightmares
and the darkness of heaven and the darkness of civilization
and the sighs of the lonely and the sighs of lovers
are indistinguishable
on the banks of brook avenue
where childhood is idyllic
and the world could not be more beautiful

Bibliography: Previous Publications

avenue b, 14th street, looking south
You Are Here: New York City Streets in Poetry. P & Q Press. 2006.
Z Miscellaneous. Winter 1989.

the beach beneath the bridge
North Coast Review. Issue 7, 1995.

the fountain of youth
The Prose Poem: An International Journal. Vol. 2, 1993.

the gambling leaguers
The Glacier Stopped Here: an anthology of poems by Dane County writers. Dane County Cultural Affairs Commission & Isthmus Publishing. 1994.

grandfather: a photograph
The Spirit That Moves Us. Vol. 6, no. 1, 1981.

justice
Live Lines: Is There a Place for Poetry in Your World? Pearson Canada Inc. 2011.
And Justice For All. Perfection Learning Company. 2000.
Welcome to Your Life: Writings for the Heart of Young America. Milkweed Editions. 1998.

lost again on old subways
Tokens: Contemporary Poetry of the Subway. P & Q Press. 2003.

***ne cede malis:* poem for the seal of the borough of the bronx**
The Bronx County Historical Society Journal. Vol. XLV, nos. 1 & 2, spring/fall 2008.

on the coping
Dusty Dog. Vol. 2, no. 1, January 1991.

standing upon the fordham road bridge
Connections: New York City Bridges in Poetry. P & Q Press. 2012.
North Coast Review. Issue 7, 1995.

triborough bridge: suspension
POETS on the line. No. 3, spring 1996.

yankee kitchen
This is an elaboration of a short poem, **genghis khan,** which appeared in *Wormwood Review.* Vol. 33, no. 3, 1993.

www.ingramcontent.com/pod-product-compliance
Lightning Source LLC
Chambersburg PA
CBHW070314240426
43663CB00038BA/2277